CONCILIUM

CONCILIUM
ADVISORY COMMITTEE

REGINA AMMICHT-QUINN	GERMANY
MARÍA PILAR AQUINO	USA
MILE BABIĆ OFM	BOSNIA–HERZEGOVINA
JOSÉ OSCAR BEOZZO	BRAZIL
WIM BEUKEN	BELGIUM
MARIA CLARA BINGEMER	BRAZIL
LEONARDO BOFF	BRAZIL
ERIK BORGMAN OP	HOLLAND
CHRISTOPHE BOUREUX OP	FRANCE
LISA SOWLE CAHILL	USA
JOHN COLEMAN	USA
EAMONN CONWAY	IRELAND
MARY SHAW COPELAND	USA
ENRICO GALAVOTTI	ITALY
DENNIS GIRA	FRANCE
NORBERT GREINACHER	GERMANY
GUSTAVO GUTIÉRREZ OP	PERU
HILLE HAKER	USA
HERMANN HÄRING	GERMANY
LINDA HOGAN	IRELAND
DIEGO IRRARÁZAVAL CSC	CHILE
WERGNER G. JEANROND	SWEDEN
JEAN-PIERRE JOSSUA OP	FRANCE
MAUREEN JUNKER-KENNY	IRELAND
FRANÇIOS KABASELE LUMBALA	DEMOCRATIC REPUBLIC OF CONGO
HANS KARL-JOSEPH KUSCHEL	GERMANY
SOLANGE LEFEBVRE	CANADA
MARY-JOHN MANANZAN	PHILIPPINES
DANIEL MARGEURAT	SWITZERLAND
ALBERTO MELLONI	ITALY
NORBERT METTE	GERMANY
DIETMAR MIETH	GERMANY
JÜRGEN MOLTMANN	GERMANY
PAUL D. MURRAY	UK
SAROJINI NADAR	(SOUTH AFRICA)
TERESA OKURE	NIGERIA
AGBONKHIANMEGHE OROBATOR SJ	KENYA
ALOYSIUS PIERIS SJ	SRI LANKA
SUSAN A. ROSS	USA
GIUSEPPE RUGGIERI	ITALY
LÉONARD SANTEDI KINKUPI	DEMOCRATIC REPUBLIC OF CONGO
SILVIA SCATENA	ITALY
PAUL SCHOTSMANS	BELGIUM
ELISABETH SCHÜSSLER FIORENZA	USA
JOHN SOBRINO SJ	EL SALVADOR
JANET MARTIN SOSKICE	UK
LUIZ CARLOS SUSIN OFM	BRAZIL
ELSA TAMEZ	COSTA RICA
CHRISTOPH THEOBALD SJ	FRANCE
ANDRÉS TORRES QUIERUGA	SPAIN
DAVID TRACEY	USA
ROBERTO TUCCI	ITALY
MARCIANO VIDAL	SPAIN
JÕAO J. VILA-CHÃ SJ	PORTUGAL
MARIE-THERES WACKER	GERMANY
ELAIN M. WAINWRIGHT	NEW ZEALAND
FELIX WILFRED	INDIA
ELLEN VAN WOLDE	HOLLAND
CHRISTOS YANNARÁS	GREECE
JOHANNES ZIZIOULAS	TURKEY

CONCILIUM

The End of Life: Making Sense of Our Finitude

Edited by

Margareta Gruber, Linda Hogan,
Stefanie Knauss

Published in 2021 by SCM Press, 3rd Floor, Invicta House, 108–114 Golden Lane, London EC1Y 0TG.

SCM Press is an imprint of Hymns Ancient & Modern Ltd (a registered charity) 13A Hellesdon Park Road, Norwich NR6 5DR, UK

Copyright © International Association of Conciliar Theology, Madras (India)

www.concilium.in

English translations copyright © 2021 Hymns Ancient & Modern Ltd.

All rights reserved. No part of this publication may be reproduced, stored in a retrieval system, or transmitted, in any form or by any means, electronic, mechanical, photocopying or otherwise, without the prior written permission of the Board of Directors of Concilium.

ISBN 978-0-334-03161-1

Concilium is published in March, June, August, October, December

Contents

Editorial	7
End-of-Life: A Religious Studies Perspective DOUGLAS JAMES DAVIES	14
The End of Life: A Perspective from Biblical Theology DIETMAR MIETH	25
(Not) The End: From Death to Life in East Asian Films KRIS H.K. CHONG	35
Health Care Practice at the End of Life: Addressing Opposite Attitudes and Diverse Contexts ANDREA VICINI	45
The End of Life in a Global Health Perspective ALEXANDRE A. MARTINS	56
Assisted Suicide: A Rational Option or a Tragedy? JEAN-PIERRE WILS	66
The Filipino Family and Health Care Decision-making at the End of Life ERIC MARCELO O. GENILO	77
Muslim Beliefs about Death: From Classical Formulations to Modern Applications ABDULAZIZ SACHEDINA	86

Ars Vivendi: Spirituality for the End of Life in
the 21st century 97
MARÍA MARCELA MAZZINI

Everything Called In Question: When a Pet is Fatally Ill 104
TAMAR A. AVRAHAM

Theological Forum 111

Sobre Hans Küng (19/03/1928 – 06/04/2021) 113
JOSÉ OSCAR BEOZZO

The Catholic Bishops of Canada Apologize to the
Indigenous Peoples of the Land 118
MICHEL ANDRAOS

The Synodal Path in Germany: An Interim Report at
Half-Time 125
STEFAN ORTH

Contributors 131

Editorial

The End of Life: Framing and Complicating the Question

The end of life seems to be a deceptively simple concept: does not the life of each being – human and other-than-human – end at some point? Is not the experience of finitude part of existence? All life has a beginning, and all life has an end. Yet the longer one thinks about this simple fact of life, the more complex it becomes, and the more questions arise, some of which are explored in this volume of Concilium.

In spite of its presence in all life, the end of life is not always consciously reflected. Indeed, in some cultural contexts – perhaps especially in the Global North – it tends to be repressed and hidden, or to be managed by "specialists" in care facilities or hospitals. Yet, in other parts of the world, as well as for poor and marginalized populations in the North, where life is a struggle against poverty, diseases or war, and where death is always present, the end of life is quite immediately a part of life. It is a part of life that comes too early and often violently, and this changes how the end of life is considered, and what questions are raised in its regard, as **Alexandre Martins'** contribution shows, which examines end-of-life challenges faced by the marginalized, in particular Indigenous peoples.

Perhaps the global COVID-19 pandemic has altered this dichotomy and made the end of life most concrete as a reality that all beings face, in many of its facets: images of rows of coffins in Italy and of funerary pyres in India have made the end of life tangible. The pandemic made it necessary to adjust many practices surrounding the end of life – accompanying the dying person, sharing grief and mourning together with family and friends, religious or other funerary rites –, and their importance became acutely felt when they were no longer possible to enact together. Even more

Editorial

importantly the injustices and exclusions that have "invisibly" marked societies have become even more obvious as we see how they impact the end of life in terms of access to care, social safety nets, or safe working conditions. It is not surprising, then, that several of the contributions in this volume draw on the experiences of the pandemic in different contexts in their reflections on the end of life (e.g. **Andrea Vicini** in his reflections on the different health care challenges in the Global North and South, **Eric Genilo's** considerations of decision-making processes surrounding the end of life in the Philippines, or the contribution by Martins mentioned above).

But what is the end of life, exactly? Is it the final endpoint of life – death –, an abrupt end, something to be avoided, fought as an enemy with all bio-technological means possible, as it is often perceived in the medical profession? Is the end of life a war zone? Or is death as the end of life more of a pause (as Vicini reflects in his contribution, drawing on the 2001 film *Wit* by Mike Nichols)? Is it not so much the end as a passage into something different? Perhaps even a new beginning? Many religious traditions have attempted to make sense of the end of life in such terms so that the end of life is understood not as an ending but as a transformation, or re-birth in death. Or perhaps, the end of life is not a point in time – the endpoint of time – at all but a period of time? One that might stretch over weeks, months or even years? **Dietmar Mieth's** reflections on the end of life as experienced in the process of aging suggests this understanding. Is the end of life then perhaps even already present in its beginning?

Each of these different ways of thinking about the end of life brings its own questions. If the end of life is identified with death, the question of how to define death, and how to recognize that it has occurred, becomes important. In this context medical indicators of death might conflict with religious or cultural ones, and create tensions, as discussed for example by **Abdulaziz Sachedina** from the perspective of Islamic bioethics with regard to the question of brain death, resuscitation, or organ transplants. On the other hand, if the end of life is seen as a period in life, it refocuses the understanding of the relationship between life and death which then appear not so much as opposites but rather as connected with each other, perhaps even as a continuity, as **Kris Chong** notes in her analysis of two Chinese films dealing – each in a different way – with the end of life. This shifts the perspective on the end of life from a medical-technological-ethico-juridical one to an existential one and orients us to the question of what it means that our existence is finite, and that we are aware of our finitude. Reflecting on the end of life leads us thus into different directions: towards death (and what is beyond), and towards life; towards the meaning of an individual's life and death, towards the quality of life as well as to how death experienced. It raises questions of identity and self-understanding, as well as questions about memory and how one will be remembered by others – a central concern of the protagonist of one of the films that Chong discusses.

Yet, while the end of life is, in this sense, an intensely personal experience – the end of an individual's life –, it is also a collective experience as it affects not only the dying subject, but also their families or loved ones, and their larger community they leave behind. **Douglas Davies** notes that the end of life makes us aware that we are not so much individuals but "dividuals," in the sense of complex personhood, who live our life and end our life in a network of relationships that includes other human beings, other-than-human beings, and the environment at large. This extended understanding of self might then also impact funerary practices which increasingly, as Davies notes for the United Kingdom, attend to the environmental impact of our death, and not just our life.

This collective or social dimension of the end of life is particularly important in cultures in which the individual is primarily understood as being a part of the community, and thus ethical-existential questions concerning the individual are seen as always also affecting the collective. Genilo and Sachedina trace the consequences of this understanding of the individual-in-community with regard to decisions about the care of terminally ill patients in the Philippines and in Islamic cultures, respectively, in which issues of patient autonomy or informed consent are secondary in relation to the family's involvement in the end of the life of their loved one.

However, as the pandemic has shown – although it has always been the case –, the end of life is embedded not only in intersubjective relationships but in social institutions and political processes that impact how it is experienced and what it means. This includes various aspects, ranging from the difficult question of assisted suicide discussed by **Jean-Pierre**

Editorial

Wils in the European context, to access to basic or advanced health care, and even more fundamentally, access to basic resources like food, water and housing, as Martins notes. The end of life is a question of biopower, as Michel Foucault has theorized: the power of the sovereign (governments or even global forces) to foster (some) life and to let (others) die. Whose death is seen as acceptable, perhaps even negligible? Whose life is fought for? What life is perceived as valuable, whose isn't? The lives of Black people, Indigenous people, migrants, the lives of the poor, those in the Global South?

Thus, although a universal experience, the end of life is experienced differently in particular contexts, and the social, cultural, political, and economic questions that are raised in regards to the end of life, differ considerably depending on this context, as the contributions to this issue show. While we are all equal in death, as the Dance of Death motif of the Late Middle Ages in Europe suggests, the end of life is marked by deep inequality and injustice. Decisions over advanced treatment options for terminally ill patients, palliative care or assisted suicide, the question of euthanasia, of what constitutes a "good death," are issues that concern the elites of North and South. However the vast population of the poor and marginalized do not even have access to clean water or clean air, let alone basic health care. Their reality is one of "misthanasia," "bad death," a term coined by Dos Anjos and used by Martins to describe the unseen, premature deaths of those whose end of life is not considered worthy of reflection and whose realities are unnnoticed in bioethical discussions about patient autonomy, the refusal of treatment or the medical definitions of death. Both Martins and Vicini critique even Catholic teaching surrounding the end of life because it is a teaching from and for the Global North, one that does not consider the experiences of the poor and marginalized around the globe. This highlights and reinforces one of the themes of this volume, namely that questions of bioethics, including the question of how to understand the end of life, cannot be considered as purely questions concerning the individual, but are questions of social relevance and thus must be engaged drawing on the resources of Catholic Social Teaching with its commitments to the option for the poor, the dignity of each person, and solidarity.

Thus a range of questions emerge around the end of life: questions of

Editorial

justice and values (discussed for example by Sachedina and Vicini), of political, social and interpersonal relationships (e.g. in Martins, Chong), the experience of time (Dietmar Mieth), of aging and illness, and how to make sense of one's finitude. The end of life relates to all dimensions and aspects of existence, and yet it remains elusive and mysterious, something we know we will experience and yet cannot know. Religious traditions with their theologies and rituals have tried to make sense of this unknown-known aspect of existence: visions of the afterlife, notions of resurrection in Christianity, or the cycle of rebirth until nirwana in Buddhism each offer possibilities to think of the end of life not so much as an endpoint but as the transition towards something new or different. Thinking about the end of life also requires thinking about what constitutes life, such as the relationship between body and soul or spirit, and how these aspects of existence will end or continue. In Christianity, the person of Christ, and his life, death and resurrection are particularly significant moments of theological reflection on the meaning of the end of life, as are reflections on the relationship between this life and the afterlife, as Mieth's exploration of biblical and theological questions around the end of life shows. From a religious studies perspective, Davies suggests that the notion of gift, central to many religious traditions, might be extended to an understanding of a grace-ful relationship between an individual and their environment that extends beyond death and encourages considerations about how one's body might be reintegrated into and give back to life-giving nature through ecologically-friendly funerary practices. Spiritual practices such as the Christian ars moriendi encourage reflection on the meaning of the end of life as entering into community with Christ and, as **María Marcela Mazzini** notes in her reflections on the experience of spiritual accompaniment of terminally ill persons, can perhaps be better understood as an artful practice of life, an ars vivendi, that encourages to live one's life from its end in eternal life. With their rituals surrounding the end of life and death, religions also provide structures for those who are left behind to deal with the loss of the life of a family or community member, and to manage the associated affects of pain, sadness, and mourning at the same time as they express and formulate beliefs about the meaning of life, death, and what happens in and after death.

This theological perspective on the end of life raises another fundamental

Editorial

question that might impact ethical considerations surrounding the end of life: is life and death in the hands of God and thus taken out of human control, or is our life and death – and that of other creatures – a matter for autonomous decision? Several articles in this issue (by Sachedina, Wils, Davies, Genilo, **Tamar Avraham**) address this question and its consequences with regard to the subject of decisions at the end of life, the principles that should guide them, and how individuals and groups should deal with the approaching end of a person's or animal's life. Here, too, the question of the end of life (and who controls it) becomes a larger question of human existence, our freedom and autonomy, and our interdependence.

The end of life is often also a moment of theodicy, of encountering the painful question why a good, all-powerful God allows the suffering and death of God's creatures. Even – and especially – for those who believe that death is not the end, that the life that ends is gathered and fulfilled in the embrace of God, it is hard to negotiate the suffering and the experiences of fear, loss, sadness or anger that may come before the end of life, as well as the memories of painful or beautiful moments lived together. This can be the case not only when the one whose life is ending is a human person, but also when it is an other-than-human animal with whom one has shared a life, as Avraham's moving reflections on accompanying her cat at the end of her life within the context of the Jewish liturgical year shows. The question of "why?" remains as an open question that needs to be raised, again and again, and as we ask it, the boundaries that seem to separate the life of human beings from those of other-than-human beings are blurred and the end of life becomes a question of the end of all life.

These initial reflections show that the end of life is anything but simple and that it requires multiple perspectives to do justice to the complex questions it raises: from material aspects of physical care to abstract and immaterial notions of time and soul; from individual concerns about the meaning of one's life in the face of its end to social issues of justice and the conditions that allow all beings to live their lives well and end them well; from reflections on the meaning of autonomy and the freedom to decide over one's life to the experience of loss of control and dependency on others; from its scientific exploration to theological speculations transcending the empirical, and to the spiritual wisdom of abandoning oneself to God in the finitude of life.

Editorial

The articles gathered in this volume hope to do justice to the complexity of the end of life and approach it from a range of different perspectives. Most authors situate their reflections in a specific context and engage the questions that arise in that situation, thereby affirming the insight that while the end of life is a universal experience of all living beings, how it is experienced and how the individuals makes sense of it depends on the context. And yet, these particular concerns resonate in other contexts and may encourage a reorientation of existing discussions about the end of life to take account of issues that have so far remained hidden.

This volume concludes with a note by **Fr. José Oscar Beozzo** commemorating the life of Hans Küng, one of the founders of the journal Concilium, who passed away in April 2021. The Theological Forum also includes a contribution by **Michel Andraos** on the recent discovery of unmarked graves of Indigenous children on the grounds of former residential schools in Canada, whose lives ended too soon and under tragic circumstances, and the role of the Church, then and now. **Stefan Orth's** brief report on the status of the synodal path in Germany sheds light on some of the struggles and possibilities in this process of renewal, especially important in light of the consultation of all the faithful in preparation of the 2022 synod on synodality, announced in May 2021 by Pope Francis.

End-of-Life:
A Religious Studies Perspective

DOUGLAS JAMES DAVIES

In this article, individual end-of life issues are aligned with those of the earth's survival, both framed by ecological-environmental factors. Notions of personhood set "the individual" against "dividual" or complex identity as we consider how emotions turn ideas into values, identities, and even destinies, as ecological issues grow. Older and newer forms of animism, souls, gift or reciprocity theory, merit-making, and the question of life-sustaining narratives are explored alongside innovative forms of funeral that celebrate life more than they curate sinners.

1. Introduction

The "end of life" is an intriguingly direct yet potentially misguiding phrase – excellent as an examination question, and entirely appropriate for this chapter's religious studies perspective. Almost as a litmus test of life commitments, and despite shared issues of aging, sickness, and physical mortality, the "end-of-life" phrase easily distinguishes between religious devotees anticipating post-mortem existence as souls, resurrected selves, or transmigrating spirits, and those convinced that death is final. In essence, existence is endless for some yet terminal for others. Still, between these polarities lie other identity states that this chapter explores through the descriptive and interpretative competence of religious studies, a perspective that often appropriates ideas from established academic disciplines, especially the arts, humanities and social sciences, framed by its non-confessional position as far as any one religious tradition is concerned. This breadth challenges any scholar's eclectic competence, especially given the later twentieth century's emergence of interdisciplinary death studies, and more recent debates over reformulating religious studies as worldview studies to accommodate the competing concepts of "religion," "spirituality," "non-religion," and "secularism."[1] All of these embrace end-of-life issues at personal, regional, and global levels, while also resonating strongly with current political-ecological negotiations surrounding environmentalism and its perilous harbinger – COVID-19.

2. Death's Environmental, Existential, and Pastoral Challenges

Here, then, environmental concerns add to humanity's long-familiar alignment of existential anxiety over death with its desire for death transcendence. At the outset this takes us from care homes for the elderly to modes of corpse disposal, issues often furnishing a neglected background to busy daily life until, just now, the COVID-19 crisis throws spotlights upon them.

2.1 Care Home Paradox

The advent of older old age in developed societies is increasingly associated with sickness, the loss of mental faculties, and transformations of identity in personal and family relationships. Financial worries over the cost of care highlight the economics of life-endings while the very status of care homes, already often negatively valued by the young and healthy, surfaced in something of a guilty cultural conscience during the COVID-19 period when the old became particularly susceptible to the virus. These erstwhile marginalized institutions suddenly assumed center-stage and, ironically perhaps, partially displaced that other pre-COVID-19 concern over autonomy of life-and-death decisions focused on assisted suicide or doctor assisted death. Such phrases transform the negative idea of personal suicide, so often deemed sinful or criminal, into the positive desire for autonomy by those previously favored with a capacity to "control" their lives. Just how these issues will be handled in post-pandemic "normality" remains to be seen.

2.2 Lifestyle Legacy

It is, however, highly probable that the near future will increasingly bring environmental values to bear upon the transition from life to death, whether challenging personal funeral options or enhancing ideas of a person's ecological legacy. Many may anticipate continuation through their biological children, complemented perhaps by their online visual and spoken post-mortem presences for as long as internet facilities permit. Uploaded identity data, and "post-human" reshaping of identity may also afford forms of electricity-based death-transcendence, schemes so different from options for personal mummification. The recent interest in minimalist lifestyles[2] advocating dispersal of one's possessions in preparation for one's death,[3] adds to these ethical conundrums as the power of human imagination transforms the biological drive to survive into the cultural phenomenon of hope.

2.3 Funeral Options

Meanwhile, focusing largely on the UK, current funeral options reveal an 80% preference for cremation, a dramatic shift from the 1931 rate of 0.93%.[4] Echoing the industrial revolution, rise in urbanization, concerns over social hygiene, two world wars, a decline in the force of Christian ritual and symbolism of burial, and the attraction of portable cremated remains, cremation rates have come to offer a rough index of practical secularization. From the late nineteenth, and with increasing frequency on to the twenty-first century, cremation arose as a means of a sanitary disposing of corpses through the industrialized technology of modern society. Practically all Christian denominations, Jews, and Muslims initially opposed modern cremation before first some Protestant, and from the mid-1960s some Catholic traditions, accepted it, albeit with varying degrees of positivity, reflecting their religious, political, and aesthetic preferences. Ecclesiastical liturgies carried little or no specific theological narrative, with churches largely adapting burial rites for the new cremation option. At the personal, micro-narrative level, the portability of cremated remains with their ability to reflect personal choice of a final resting place fostered family narratives of deposition, often despite Christian ecclesiastical policy advocating their interment.

The Christian funerary narrative of burial that undergirds cremation rites and remains rooted in the theological embrace of a resurrection hope, contrasts with most Hindu-derived grand narratives of cosmic transmigration of identity-aligned life-forces moderated by the notion of karma and the effect of moral duty. Life was, traditionally, conceived in phases from the embodying of a life-force within the womb, through childhood and younger student-hood, through marriage and adulthood, into an increasing withdrawal from society that could even include a formal funeral ritual prior to biological death. The final cremation would release the life-force for its transmigration and potential reincarnation. The symbolism of cremation smoke that rises and is aligned with subsequent fertile rain falling back to earth, as also of cremated remains being consigned to flowing river waters, marks the wider integration of mortality and vitality in a cosmic flow. Over millennia, this tradition generated extensive ideological and mythical matrices.[5] But that symbolic smoke carried no such significance for nineteenth- and much of twentieth-century Christian Britain and was often shielded or hidden. Moreover, what was deemed sanitary and "green" in 1900 had developed dark ecological overtones by 2000 through cremation's noxious output and high energy input.

Reflecting these changing times in the UK, from the mid-1990s an increasing minority has been inclined towards eco-friendly woodland burial in a biodegradable container, often reflecting their desire to make a return gift to nature. Furthermore, in the 2020s some funeral providers are developing processes of body-dissolution through alkaline hydrolysis – as with the tradename Resomation – while others in the USA are investigating body-composting, all with varying degrees of ecological concern.

A further, albeit minute minority, mostly in the US, plan, at considerable expense, to have either their head or entire body processed and deep-frozen until such time as medical science takes their cryogenically preserved entities, cures their initial cause of death, and restores them to life in a future world where even cloning may reap an identity-reward.[6]

3. Life-forces
In all of this, dying and dead bodies offer social and psychological problems alongside religious, historical and philosophical issues over embodiment, experience, and the emotional dynamics of identity. Along with rites of inhumation, cremation, and memorializing the dead, ideas of a soul or life-force remain pertinent, whether in ancestor veneration in some traditional and many East Asian cultures, transmigration through

many existences in Indian-derived traditions, or the resurrection motifs of later Jewish, Christian, and Islamic worlds, and ongoing rites for those "sleeping" in death.

3.1 Animisms Old and New

Such "soul" ideas help sustain notions of enduring identity as well as providing some active agency for ongoing reciprocal relations. Over recent decades the once unfashionable notion of "animism" has received a new lease of life in studies exploring how some people, not least in traditional societies, intuit a life-force in natural phenomena, and align these in ritual-symbolic ways with human beings. The Victorian anthropologist E.B. Tylor[7] explored "animism" through ideas of the soul as a vital principle empowering human life, underlying dream experiences, leaving the body at death, and sometimes staying near the corpse as funerary rites foster its transition to the realm of ancestors. The current research of both David Kramer[8] and Matthew Suriano[9] has admirably demonstrated such soul dynamics for Hebrew Bible contexts. In many traditional cultures, taking care of the sick, departing, and newly installed ancestral souls, ensures good ongoing relationships between the living and the dead while also seeking a blessing rather than a curse. Such transition periods may last days, months, or years as the early twentieth-century anthropologist Robert Hertz[10] established with his notion of "double-burial" whose "wet phase" of corpse dissolution, and "dry phase" of skeletal remains could be aligned with emotions of grief and ongoing changes in identity of the living with their dead and of the dead with the living.

Another life-force perspective on the end of life has grown alongside reports of near-death and out-of-body experiences associated with the resuscitation of erstwhile clinically dead people. Some see these as exemplifying the reality of souls, spirits, or life-forces, while others keep open the issue of causation, as with Allan Kellehear's findings on hundreds of events preceding and surrounding a person's death.[11] His scholarly documentation of world-wide cases avoids easy reductionist explanations of, for example, chemical imbalance in dying brains. Other recent studies, often derived from anthropological fieldwork amongst traditional societies in South America, have reinvigorated issues of animism. Istvan Praet,[12] for example, seeks to understand "life" more in terms of quality of existence and social participation than in a biology of body-systems, while numerous studies of plants, trees, and fungi also reset existential issues amidst the natural environment.[13] Merlin Sheldrake's increasingly popular approach to the entangled nature of life includes a telling subtitle – "How Fungi Make Our Worlds, Change Our Minds, and Shape Our Futures."[14] This captures the current ecological and ethical dynamic that resonates with green or natural burials to which we return below.[15]

3.2 Animism and Holy Spirit

Remaining with such dynamic themes, we might well ask how religious studies might prompt theology to extend the creedal motif of the Holy Spirit as the "lord and giver of life" within this new arena, or to reconsider Albert Schweitzer's theme of "reverence for life."[16] To integrate end-of-life issues with the complexity of life, mortality, and the ongoing eco-destiny of the earth is a worthy challenge. The dust to which one Genesis myth consigns humanity might now carry a dynamism that contrasts the "dry as dust" motif of cemeteries that curate sinners, albeit hopeful ones, with the vitality of woodland burial sites. For the issue of the moral identity of the dead that pervades traditional Christian liturgies and their assumptions concerning sinful humanity awaiting eschatological transformative redemption, now increasingly contrasts with secular or merely religiously disinterested funerals that self-define as celebrations of life.

4. Life-Celebration

There are few more telling and pressing portrayals of a person's moral status within the joint religious economy of salvation and ecology of creation than those underpinning funeral liturgies. For in them the theological-ideological weight of all religions carries heavy loads of relevance for today's fragile ecology, with sin and life-celebration circling each other.

4.1 Ritual Medium and Message

In the UK and elsewhere, civil celebrants of various kinds have rapidly grown in number, often replacing priests, when giving ritual voice to this celebration of an authentic reflection of the deceased's life-practices and preferences. Much can be said about this contemporary correlation of funerals with life-orientations of the dead, including the eco-environmental worldview.[17] In this, issues of moral character and responsibility assume much wider reference than any simple balance of good and bad deeds, divine judgement, and afterlife's destiny. The widespread human desire for merit-making and status enhancement, whether in society at large or in religious domains, remains significant and capable of expression through funeral choices

Whether seeking to interpret the celebration of life in non-destiny directed modern funerals, or in traditional anticipations of a heavenly afterlife, one ready theoretical resource lies in studies of the gift by Marcel Mauss.[18] Largely rooted in the threefold mutual obligation to give, receive, and return alienable goods of a market-economy kind, Mauss's ideas are, with caution, applicable not only to Hindu-derived notions of karma but also to the treasury of merit developed in some Catholic thought. The latter's historical association with indulgences, and Protestantism's responsive focus on Christ's merit, faith, and grace helped transform the world's religious map and still influence funeral liturgies: but what of modern funeral celebrations?

4.2 Celebrating Inalienable Life

Developments of Mauss's ideas highlight a different dynamic path that links people to the deep resources of the meaning of life through sentiments symbolized in inalienable gifts.[19] Moving beyond market economies of obligation and reward, these prompt a different dynamic between persons, whether religious believers and their deity, or between folk and their environmental bonds. Having pursued these issues some years ago when discussing merit-making and salvation, and gift and charisma,[20] I would like to propose here, for the first time, another perspective on the end of life grounded in inalienability and the "celebration of life" motif of increasing numbers of funerals. Whether markedly religious, religion-disinterested, or avowedly secular, their ethos and intent embrace the dynamic of inalienable factors. Very loosely speaking, this might even be designated as a love-grace pattern of relationship between people, or between people and the environment, as well as – where appropriate – between humans and the divine. I once contrasted the eschatological fulfillment of identity typical of traditional Christianity with a retrospective fulfillment of identity more typical of a secular mind-set. There I also spoke of an ecological fulfillment of identity.[21] Now, I think we may take those ideas one step further given the increasing emergence of the ecological grand narrative, and to enhance this scenario I outline one potentially helpful way of thinking about ideas, emotions, identity, and destiny.

5. From Idea to Destiny: Grief's Pervading Emotion

This begins with the obvious point that the world is full of words – simple names for things – and the fact that life circumstances ensure that emotions pervade some words to create values. When such values contribute to our sense of identity, they constitute beliefs, and some may go on to frame a sense of destiny, allowing us to speak of "religious beliefs" or "destiny factors." Most indigenous and "world-religion" traditions deal in destiny when speaking of supernatural heavens, paradise, transmigrating life-forces, domains of punishment, purgation, and judgement.[22] But now "destiny" makes an entry through ecological-environmental concerns. Does this not make a game-change for end-of-life issues? I think it does.

It is worth noting that many, often younger, people find "death," "loss," and "mourning," to be "simply words" until they personally experience bereavement. Then "grief" is transformed from a mere word to an emotion-pervaded "value" that helps shape a person's identity. This process can extend further towards a sense of destiny as with "resurrection" for traditional Christianity and Islam, or transmigration-reincarnation for many Hindu-derived traditions. Within many traditional-indigenous groups, destiny also frames the ancestors' domain and its links with their living descendants, with myths and doctrines furnishing life supporting accounts of mutual co-existence brought into dynamic experience in ritual behavior. This approach is equally significant for the many modern contexts often described as secular. While even recently, one might have defined the secular as the demise or absence of a sense of destiny, the environmental grand narrative now militates against this. This is especially interesting once atheist regimes enter the debate, and their idealization of, say, a communist society also encounters an environmental turn.

6. Narrating Identities

All such societies and their hope-laden futures have roots in persuasive narratives. Their acceptance, and embodied appropriation can engender wisdom just as easily as their rejection may foster despair. Humanity's narrative status is constantly played out through daily gossip, family conversations, celebrity and sporting media, community myths, hagiographies, liturgical matrices, and the formal theology and science of specialists. These convey a sense of overarching meaning with religions constituting the primary and often dominant cultural means of curating death. Both through practical rituals with the body and in grand narratives of post-mortem identity, these accounts follow my formulaic pattern of ideas transformed to values through the agency of emotions. This means, for example, that religious or scientific accounts of the world may mean nothing to people until and unless some emotional addition transforms them into values. Moreover, such valued accounts sometimes become cherished frames for identity, and even of destiny. Once it was usual to speak of extensive religious narratives as salvation histories, and, for millions, their very excitement and force still foster an enhanced identity, frequently moving it into that sense of ultimate significance – or destiny.

Given today's increasing demand for ecology to engage populations, it may be that "science" needs attractive grand narratives much as religions do. In some religiously conservative Christian areas "science" is deemed to be just some "theory," as in the "theory of evolution," while the gospel is an emotionally absorbing drama of salvation. This is highly significant just now as many religious traditions wake up not so much to "heaven" and individual future life, but to the viable human habitation of the earth. It is of considerable significance that, unlike even James Lovelock and his Gaia theory of 1990s,[23] the current emergence of Richard Attenborough and Greta Thunberg mark those who speak of and embody the emotional concern over human survival and ecological destiny. Although Richard Dawkins, for example, had come to be seen by some as embodying an atheist scientific tale of existence, much environmental science had largely lacked embodying celebrities. Perhaps the very "impersonal" character of "science" has counted against emotional attraction of people at large to scientific "theories" and practice, but times are changing, catalyzed perhaps by the COVID-19 crisis. It is no accident that some countries have spotlighted celebrities when they received their vaccination, allying them with the grand narrative of vaccination and social duty. Religions probably need their own eco-warriors.

7. The Ecological Grand Narrative: The Environmental Canopy

Our times demand the mobilization of grand narrators across the religious-secular-destiny continuum who embody and proclaim this emergent era of ecology and environmentalism. The older sociological idea of religion as a sacred canopy can now also consider the need for an "environmental canopy."[24] This grand narrative of ecology-environmentalism offers benefits in fostering emotions to enhance personal identity and world-wide destiny. Following the ideas-destiny trajectory, this environmental canopy would readily attract a complex interplay of anxiety and fear over the survival of human populations mixed with an idealistic hope of world-wide collaboration in halting global warming. Certainly, as already intimated, environmentalism is increasingly influencing funeral agencies, burial and cremation authorities, government concern, and many individuals, too. Death's carbon footprints are becoming more visible. While the time has come for political-economic discourse to advocate the inalienable factors within ecological concerns with "life" itself, should not religious traditions also foster similar inalienable values? What are the theological insights into forms of love-grace dynamics of funerary framings of environmental grand narratives?

8. Narrative and Dividual Personhood

However we interpret our present situation in 2020–2021, the fact of the COVID-19 pandemic has prompted its own grand narrative of peril, grief, and survival, involving a dramatic shift of existential emphasis from the once favored "individual" of much western philosophy and sociology, to a far more collective sense of identity. The commitment of medical personnel, armies of volunteers, and open scientific collaboration invites a new account of collaborative personhood. So, too, with the very issue of end-of-life care, something that I began to outline before the COVID-19 crisis with the notion of "dividual" or complex personhood that challenges the western emphasis upon the individual and its postmodern near-obsession with a relatively isolated self.[25] For not only is my personhood constituted of the many who have helped "form" me, but also of the "animated" environment nurturing us all. Even a slight shift in our grammar of discourse of identity can affect ethical and social policies while also touching our wider perception of destiny.

Douglas James Davies

Notes

1. André Droogers/Anton van Harskamp, *Methods for the Study of Religious Change: From Religious Studies to Worldview Studies*, Sheffield: Equinox, 2014.
2. James Wallman, *Stuffocation: Living More with Less*, New York: Penguin, 2015.
3. Margareta Magnusson, *The Gentle Art of Swedish Death Cleaning: How to Free Yourself and Your Family from a Lifetime of Clutter*, New York: Scribner, 2017.
4. Douglas J. Davies with Lewis H. Mates, "Cremation Statistics," in Douglas J. Davies with Lewis H. Mates (eds.), *The Encyclopedia of Cremation*, Aldershot: Ashgate, 2005, 431–456.
5. Jonathan Parry, *Death in Banaras*, Cambridge: Cambridge University Press, 1994.
6. Robert C. W. Ettinger, *The Prospect of Immortality*, edited by Charles Tandy, Palo Alto: Ria University Press, 2005.
7. Edward Burnet Tylor, *Primitive Culture*, Cambridge: Cambridge University Press, 1971.
8. David Kraemer, *The Meanings of Death in Rabbinic Judaism*, London: Routledge, 2000.
9. Matthew Suriano, *History of Death in the Hebrew Bible*, Oxford: Oxford University Press, 2018.
10. Robert Hertz, "A Contribution to the Study of the Collective Representation of Death," in Rodney Needham/Claudia Needham (eds.), *Death and the Right Hand*, New York: Free Press, 29–86, here 77.
11. Allan Kellehear, *Visitors at the End of Life: Finding Meaning and Purpose in Near-death Phenomena*, New York: Columbia University Press, 2020.
12. Istvan Praet, *Animism and the Question of Life*, London: Routledge, 2013.
13. Matthew Hall, *Plants as Persons: A Philosophical Botany*, New York: State University of New York Press, 2011.
14. Merlin Sheldrake, *Entangled Life: How Fungi Make Our Worlds, Change Our Minds, and Shape Our Futures*, London: Bodley Head, 2020.
15. Ken West, *A Guide to Natural Burial*, London: Shaw and Sons, 2010.
16. Albert Schweitzer, *My Life and Thought*, translated by C.T. Campion, London: Allen & Unwin, 1933.
17. Douglas Davies/Hannah Rumble, *Natural Burial: Traditional-Secular Spiritualities and Funeral Innovation*, London: Continuum, 2012.
18. Marcel Mauss, *The Gift: Forms and Functions of Exchange in Archaic Societies*, translated by I. Cunnison, London: Cohen and West, 1966. See also, Wendy James/N.J. Allen (eds.), *Marcel Mauss: A Centenary Tribute*, New York: Berghahn, 1998.
19. Maurice Godelier, *The Enigma of the Gift*, Oxford: Blackwell, 1999.
20. Douglas Davies, *Anthropology and Theology*, Oxford: Berg, 2002, 53–80, 195–210.
21. Douglas Davies, *A Brief History of Death*, Oxford: Blackwell, 2005, 118–126.
22. Douglas Davies, *Death, Ritual and Belief: The Rhetoric of Funerary Rites*, third edition, London: Bloomsbury, 2017, 4–10.
23. James Lovelock, *The Ages of Gaia: A Biography of our Living Earth*, New York: Norton, 1995.
24. Pace Peter Berger, *The Sacred Canopy*, London: Faber, 1969.
25. Douglas J. Davies, "Dividual Identity in Grief Theories, Palliative and Bereavement Care," *Palliative Care and Social Practice* 14 (2020), 1–12.

The End of Life: A Perspective from Biblical Theology

DIETMAR MIETH

In Western societies we are aware of points of disruption: disruption in the feeling of failing strength in old age, illness, weakness, infirmity and death. Passive surrender to God – as creator and giver of life in all its earthly states – is replaced by an autonomous judgment of what makes life possible and worth living, and an autonomous decision about death.

Christianity, together with the other Abrahamic religions, takes more into account, a transformation of death into life. This transformation of death has a retroactive effect on our view of earthly life and death. The transformation in advance of earthly life into dying back and isolation places earthly life under the spell of heavenly expectation. Suffering brings us to God. This article both presents this tradition of the mors mystica and criticises its individual interpretation and its passivity.

When we think of the 'end of life' we often think of dying and death. For many people on earth the end of life is abrupt. They die as victims in war, as victims of oppression and violence, snatched away by an epidemic, or of hunger and thirst.[1] Human life is ended before it could reflect on itself.

In rich, mainly Western, countries the 'age' at which the 'end of life' begins is today shifting into the seventieth year of life. It is totally different in the regions of the world plagued by crises and hunger. There, people are still dying before they really come to life. Early death, caused by human beings or simply accepted, also belongs to 'the end of life'. It is all repeated, intensified in many different ways. It is as though our hands that scoop up water grew and became broader, but still the water continued to run through our fingers. What happens to the life that runs through our hands? On the one hand we can look at old age and develop a theology about it, as the theological ethicist Alfons Auer has done.[2] Alternatively we can focus on the fact that our issue is a time of earthly life, but also at the same time about life itself. Is life more than 'time and space'? At the heart of the Christian faith is the mystery of a divine sharing in our life and death (see Phil 2. 5-11), an unquestioning descent into hate, pain and death. This mystery is certainly part of the last topic we can do theology on here, and leads us into the consolations at the end of the book of Revelation.

But the end of life as 'time' is clearly experienced and reflected on in the Old Testament's tradition of biblical theology. This experience of the end of life, on the one hand as the limiting of the lifetime of the person and on the other as its extension through the community that comes after in time, should not be so easily dissolved into God's all-embracing saving action.

A further experience: there is life not just *at* the end of life, but also *in* the end of life. There are the starving whose life goes on in hunger. There are those suffering in epidemics, who live in the expectation of death. There are the diseases that can today be treated in a way that prolongs life and can be endured. There is the fading away of the music of life in old age.

In the rest of this article I present various ways of looking at the question that may be helpful here: (1) the continuing life of the community, which takes us beyond 'I live and die' and is especially emphasised in the Old Testament; (2) the scream of protest against senseless suffering and death, which begins at an early date in the psalms and continues in today's religious music; (3) the impulse to save life out of 'compassion'; (4) death in old age; (5) a spirituality of *ars moriendi*, 'the art of dying', and (6) of *ars vivificandi*, 'the art of giving life', as a practice of transforming the attitude towards life as a search for justice. I shall not here discuss autonomous judgment and decisions at the end of life.[3]

1. The end of life and the community
'Whoever chooses life will live and grow old,' we find written in the book of Deuteronomy (Dt 30.19-20). 'Life' here means life in 'the Word of God', in commandment and promise. 'This is no trifling matter for you, but rather your very life' (Dt 32.47).[4] What is promised here is on the one

hand an extension of the length of life, and on the other the prolongation of the community life beyond death, that is the continuity of the family, the surviving community and 'people' of God. In other words, 'life' here expands, as it were, in concentric circles. To summarise the message of super-individual maintenance of life, here I choose the word 'community', because since the promises to Abraham life is also linked to 'land' (see Gen 13.14-17), and with descendants (see Gen 15 and 18), but also with the survival of a community, as God promises 'to preserve a numerous people' (Gen 50.20).[5]

So it is clear to believers that life and death come from God. God is the Lord of life because he is the one who remains for ever the same: that is one of the possible translations of Ex 3.14 ('I am who I am'). Community life is ordered by divine instructions: 'Those who keep the commandment will live' (Prov 19.16). Pursuing justice means finding life (cf Prov 22.4). The person who directs their life by the commandments, who does right and upholds it, that person is just and 'shall surely live' (Ezek 18.9). In contrast, we may also hear: 'Jealousy and anger shorten life' (Sir 30.24). It is true that the life of the person who fears God may involve 'sufferings', but there is always the promise in the sense of community continuity, even at the end of the book of Job.

Can we draw conclusions from these very general but hardly controvertible findings? I think we can draw the following conclusions: (1) life is thought of in these texts in very 'this-worldly' terms; (2) the way life 'departs' from a person is very close to what a person does or fails to do; (3) the reward for such a life is neatly summed up, not only in heavenly promises, but also in what is required for survival (land, water, etc.) and community life.

These are three aspects that I would like to offer as an alternative to what has become an intense Christian spiritual 'otherworldliness'. Jesus' instructions and promises as he preached on his journeys can also be brought into a 'this-worldly' context: in Matthew 5, Jesus promises a model of society, land ownership (see Mt 5.5), eating one's fill and reconciliation; after the sermon on the mount comes the promise of 'daily bread' (Mt 6.11), freedom from worry (Mt 6. 25-34) and a long life (Mt 6.27). And if we connect this with the original promise in Mark 10.28-30, we are explicitly told that for the radical keeping of the commandment and the following of Jesus' way of life what seems to have been lost will be repaid 'a hundredfold now in this present age...with persecutions and in the age to come'. Is this a Jesuanic foretelling of the medieval monasteries born out of the poverty of wandering preachers that then became rich? I prefer to think that we can connect Jesus' promise to Old Testament 'thisworldliness' and use it as an argument against letting that be forgotten, so that 'thisworldliness' remains a Christian obligation that must not be dissolved into 'heaven'.

Sensitivity to the sufferings of others is an implication of the gospels (see especially Matthew 25). The life of the early Christian communities, even if the picture we have is idealised, the foundation of Christian hospitals or infirmaries in the late Roman empire, the founding of the knights hospitallers and many other institutions, such as in recent times the hospice movement, are all signs along the path of the this-worldly obligation, assumed by towns or communities, to help shape the end of life. This concern is not simply defined in relation to the end-point of dying and death.

Martyrdom in primitive Christianity did not have the sense of earning heaven by shortening life, but of confessing the faith. Christendom was constructed in churches, monasteries and hospitals. As it almost completely permeated society in the middle ages, these sites of charity marked the image of cities: an image on the way to the 'holy city Jerusalem'. Nevertheless the very general concept of human dignity that prevailed in the middle ages and in humanism did not reach its moral profile until the Enlightenment, the movement for democracy and the definition of human rights.

2. Protest against meaningless suffering and death

The presence of religions has a different appearance today from what the Western European retreat from the churches would lead us to suppose. The global world is centred differently in the post-colonial period, and in this sense it is also post-European. In Europe we are beginning no longer to think of ourselves as engaged in a foreign 'mission', but to reflect on the original religious backflows that are reaching us. The cry of the oppressed remains and merges with the cry of those tortured by Church and state in the process of European expansion.

The End of Life: A Perspective from Biblical Theology

But the secular tradition also has religion and the outcry it produced as part of its inheritance. A poet who tried to capture and express this cry at the end of life was Ingeborg Bachmann. This quotation is from her '*Lieder auf der Flucht*' ('Songs in Flight', 1956)[6]:

> But I lie alone,
> covered in ice
> wounded all over.
> The snow has not yet
> Bound my eyes.
> The dead, pressed against me,
> Are silent in all languages.
> No-one loves me or has
> Swung a lamp in my honour.

This poem bears a close resemblance to Psalm 88:

> For my soul is full of troubles,
>   and my life draws near to Sheol.
> I am counted among those who go down to the Pit;
>   I am like those who have no help,
> like those forsaken among the dead,
>   like the slain that lie in the grave,
> like those whom you remember no more,
>   for they are cut off from your hand.
> You have put me in the depths of the Pit,
>   in the regions dark and deep.
> Your wrath lies heavy upon me,
>   and you overwhelm me with all your waves.
> You have caused my companions to shun me;
>   you have made me a thing of horror to them.
> I am shut in so that I cannot escape.
>   (vs. 3-9)

The closeness of the psalm to Job's denunciation of God (Job 30) cannot be overlooked. In Bachman, accusation is also part of the personal complaint. She can also put this in less individual terms, when on Good

Friday she thinks of the murdered Jews: in her image of God, with the raised, commanding hand, the two figures used to swear an oath are missing.

Such protests can be contextualised, but the cannot be eliminated. 'Why does a good God let us suffer?', many believers ask. We do not know how and in what form God finally manifests himself, say such diverse texts as the book of Job (Job 38-39) or Meister Eckhart, when he insists that God's goodness cannot be grasped by our judgments.

Our unknowing, the lack of calculability, stretches into the end of life. That also applies to the end of an individual life as much as to the victims who cannot reflect on the end of life. It also applies to the limitation of our clarification of faith through philosophy, which nevertheless is our task in theology. This task can only be attempted practically, in active compassion with those who are suffering and dying.

3. Compassion, the Christian impulse to action[7]

Johann Baptist Metz chose 'compassion' as an expression for 'active sensitivity to suffering'.[8] He associated with the concept a 'deep structure of anamnesis', that is, a remembrance that works against forgetting, an ethic of listening obedience to the authority of suffering in the figure of the Servant of God and a 'political' 'open-eyed' mysticism of suffering. I have described this as laying the political foundations of an 'ethic of sympathy'.[9] The practical implications of this are already contained in the parable of the Good Samaritan (Lk 10.25-37), which is the basis of the Christian almshouse and hospice movement. The man who fell into the hands of robbers faces the 'end of life' if no help is given to him. The parable says that there are no legitimate grounds for 'seeing and passing by', not even religious grounds.[10] The Samaritan places no temporal or material limits on his help. This willingness to respond is a virtue that we also call *misericordia*, compassion. Saving life takes priority over the accompaniment of dying.

4. Death in old age[11]

When we think of 'old age' in this connection, the beginning of the 'end of life' is today sliding forward to the age of 70. Death in old age as the end of life is different according to the circumstances, whether it takes place when a person 'has had enough of life' or is felt to be a 'premature' end of a life with a lot to look forward to or expectations of changes in the future. In old age as a final experience, expectation is replaced by memory. In other words, we no longer live looking forwards but looking backwards. In contrast, time speeds up, moving forwards, tomorrow comes faster and if you lose track of time and then catch up, you wonder where the time went. And despite all one's efforts you are no longer in time with other people, but increasingly felt by yourself and others to be 'once upon a time'.

Remembering now no longer produces temporal distance, but immediate presence, as though everything you remember had happened only yesterday or a little earlier. In the process what you remember is not only consciously present as something that happened, risen out of 'lost time', it is felt as in the present, so that you feel a 'feeling of feeling'. Time no longer moves in a line that stretches out straight, but lies in spirals of remembering – with a slight overlapping or superimposition – and these spirals in their centre allow you to see through into a depth at their heart – an abyss. So, as you feel it, at least, you come to the ground of life.

Now the end of this life has really come nearer in its unavoidability. I may try to delay it, but that makes no difference to the fact that when it happens, that 'then' will be no different from now. That is why accompaniment starts now. You talk, calculate and plan for death for much longer. What does that mean? An anticipation of the end-experience begins. What happened to me, what is happening to me, what will happen to me? I am now no longer the ordinary person who asks where they come from and where they're going, but I am either losing myself or winning myself in death.[12]

5. *Ars moriendi – mors mystica*[13]

A person who wishes to go beyond death already comes close to death beforehand in thinking and feeling. That is the principle of the *ars moriendi*, that is, the art of meeting death in life through a process of self-education that takes away death's sting. A person who denies the 'world' in the sense of temporality, multiplicity and bodiliness *(negatio)* has nothing more to lose in losing life in this world. 'Those who lose their life will keep it,' says Jesus (Lk 17.33). It would be a misunderstanding to take this in a physical sense. The point is much more 'to be as though they had not' (see 1 Cor 7.29-30), that is, to find, through an inner independence that a withdrawal of self can bring from needs, wishes and desires, a way of living that rests in itself. That means that in fact already 'in this age' (Mk 10.30 – the Greek word translated 'age' is *kairos*, 'moment' or 'opportunity') a space of freedom from hardships, though not a complete one, comes into being. Nevertheless because the burdens to be borne are less, this will lead to a greater feeling of happiness.

Mors mystica (literally, 'mystical death') means nothing more than placing this question in a religious context and trying to live on these terms. That can be done through a bringing forward of the experience of dying by 'dying' to things, relationships, all sorts of demands, through giving one's life for a conviction or – in a life-saving act – for others. The first option leads to asceticism as *mors mystica*, the second to martyrdom, the third to taking the place of someone else. In the history of Jesus all these options are discussed and united.

The tradition of *mors mystica* in Christianity is diverse. We can start with Paul, dying with Christ (see Rom 6.8-14; 8.13) and his longing 'to depart and be with Christ' (Phil 1. 21-23). His anticipation of death consists of a double feeling, being in 'the sufferings of this present time' (see Rom 8.18) and at the same time to be hoping for future glory (see also Rom 5.2). This was later developed as a teaching about monastic life. A life of prayer is a life of anticipation. A life of ascesis is a training of the mind to be 'in the world but not of the world'. But in a stricter sense *mors mystica* is a sinking into the abyss of God, as, for example, Mechthild of Magdeburg describes it. Her 'alienation from God' describes the feeling of the difference between the distance she feels and the closeness she needs.[14] For the women mystics the 'no' of the rejection of 'nothings' becomes an acceptance of their own nothingness and so to a feeling of being held in an inaccessible grasp in which no one can ever again trouble them.

6. *Ars vivificandi:* 'Getting up' in the face of death and the anticipation of the Kingdom of God as justice

Some of Meister Eckhart's sermons also make a link between 'getting up' and 'resurrection', in which the former signifies dealing with life 'now'. In other words, the resurrection is already understood in spiritual and practical terms as implementing in life rising with Christ (*si consurrexistis cum Christo*) in the sense of Colossians 3.1.[15] Here the preacher says jokingly: 'A lot of people get up together, but they don't rise with Christ.'[16] But that's the point: what is to rise is ours.[17] But this anticipation of the resurrection has not only an individual, but also a social meaning. With justice we are on the way to the Omega point as the 'end of life'.[18]

The Tübingen theologian Johann Sebastian Drey (1777–1853) regards the Kingdom of God as the advance proclamation of a new life in community. In so doing he steers our vision towards the ethical sphere of life, justice and community, also understood as an 'afterlife of the dead'. Incarnation thus becomes a universal task for all human beings. It is the 'inclusivity' implicit in the Christian concept of God's incarnation, though not an idea to base missionary activity on. Nevertheless the correlation God – justice – and the human being as just gives rise, in theological terms, to divine recognition of every human being as human. This also gives the 'end of life' a perspective that we may call, with Teilhard de Chardin, who inserts the paradigm of evolution, the Omega perspective.

Translated by Francis McDonagh

Notes

1. See Jean-Pierre Wils, *Das Nachleben der Toten: Philosophie auf der Grenze*, Paderborn, 2019, pp 63–69 on 'death and violence' and 'the brutalisation of death'.
2. See Alfons Auer, *Geglücktes Altern: Eine theologisch-ethische Ermutigung*, Freiburg, 1995.
3. But, in addition to the article in this issue, see: Dietmar Mieth and Irene Mieth, Sterben und Lieben: *Selbstbestimmung bis zuletzt*, Freiburg, 2019; Jacques Pohier, *La mort opportune: Les droits des vivants sur la fin de leur vie*, Paris, 1998; Jean-Pierre Wils, *Ars moriendi: Über das Sterben*, Frankfurt, 2007.
4. 'Choose life so that you and your descendants may live…for that means life to you and length of days'. (Dt 30.19-20, NRSV)
5. I am aware that this attempt to find a concept that isn't based on anonymous societies is open to challenge, but it is difficult to find an expression in this context that is not open to misunderstanding.
6. For a detailed exposition, see: Irene Mieth and Dietmar Mieth, '"Allein im Eisverhau" – Psalmen finden in Gedichten', in Gottfried Bitter and Norbert Mette (ed.), *Leben mit Psalmen: Entdeckungen und Vermittlungen*, Munich, 1983, pp 53–61.
7. See Johann Baptist Metz, Lothar Kuld, and Adolf Weisbrod, *Compassion: Weltprogramm des Christentums. Soziale Verantwortung lernen*, Freiburg, 2000.
8. Metz, Kuld and Weisbrod, *Compassion*, pp 13-17.
9. Metz, Kuld and Weisbrod, *Compassion*, pp 21-25.

10. This also has serious implications for dealing with abuse in the Catholic Church and the structures that made it possible.
11. On this, see Auer, *Geglücktes Altern: Eine theologisch-ethische Ermutigung*.
12. Meister Eckhart develops these thoughts in his Sermon 109; see Meister Eckhart, *Predigten*, Deutsche Werke vol. 4.2, edited and translated by Georg Steer, Stuttgart, 2003–2019, Sermon 109, pp 761–774. English edition: *The Complete Mystical Works of Meister Eckhart*, trans. and ed. by Maurice O'C Walshe, rev. by Bernard McGinn, New York, 2009).
13. See Alois M. Haas, 'Mors mystica, ein mystologisches Motiv', in: Alois M. Haas, *Sermo mysticus: Studien zu Theologie und Sprache der deutschen Mystik*, Fribourg, 1979, pp 392–480. Haas provides a comprehensive survey from Bernard of Clairvaux to the German Dominican mystics. A critical view of the *ars moriendi* can be found in Wils, *Das Nachleben der Toten: Philosophie auf der Grenze*, pp 211–215.
14. See Mechthild von Magdeburg, *Das fließende Licht der Gottheit*, bilingual edition, translations by Gisela Vollmann-Profe, Berlin, 2010, Book IV, Chap. 12, 258–260. An English edition is Mechthild of Magdeburg, *Flowing Light of the Divinity* translated by Christiane Mesch Galvani; edited, with an introduction, by Susan Clark, Shrewsbury, MA, 1990.
15. See Meister Eckhart, *Predigten, Deutsche Werke vol. 2*, edited and translated by Josef Quint, Stuttgart, 1988, Sermon 35, 173–175.
16. Meister Eckhart, Sermon 35, 175,4.
17. Meister Eckhart, Sermon 35, 176,4.
18. See Dietmar Mieth, 'Die Gerechtigkeit des Reiches Gottes als sozialtheologisches Motiv', in: Dietmar Mieth (ed.), *Solidarität und Gerechtigkeit: Die Gesellschaft von morgen gestalten*, Stuttgart, 2009, pp 35–61 (referring to Johann Sebastian Drey).

(Not) The End: From Death to Life in East Asian Films

KRIS H.K. CHONG

The most common cinematic representation of the end of human lives is physical death, whether natural or otherwise. This article, however, moves away from the dominant notion of "death as cessation" and explores the religious sensibilities attached to the depiction of death in the mainland Chinese film Getting Home *(Zhang Yang, 2008) and the Tibetan Buddhist film* Balloon *(Pema Tseden, 2019). In contrast to the western concept of "rest in peace," which alludes to the soul finding peace in eternal heaven, death in* Getting Home *shows the cultural notion of returning to one's birthplace, whereas in* Balloon, *death is a means to rebirth.*

1. Introduction
Life and death are not always polar opposites, but a meaningful life-death paradox to be unpacked in different contexts. In cinematic representations, death occupies a central role as the binding force that filmmakers employ to capture relationships in communities and to depict the manner in which the characters contrive to make sense of their lives. In the following analysis, I will explore how the characters in *Getting Home* (Zhang Yang, 2008) and *Balloon* (Pema Tseden, 2019), within the expanse of their unique actions and religious beliefs, experience death not as an ending, but as both a meaningful continuation of life and the pathway that leads to a new beginning.

Through the lens of Chinese cultural/religious traditions that emphasize the importance of returning to one's birthplace for burial, we see in *Getting Home* how the protagonist painstakingly lugs his friend's dead body over a long distance to ensure it returns to its roots, the friend's hometown.

Along the way, we observe a bizarre funeral held by a childless man, driven by his Confucian values of family relationships. Drawing on the Tibetan Buddhist imagination, where death is not about the termination of earthly life, but about the dead living on in both the memories and body of the living, Balloon is a contemplation of the ineffable mysticism of the continuity of life.

2. Getting Home

Film critics often dub mainland Chinese director Zhang Yang's award-winning film *Getting Home* as a black comedy depicting the clash of values in contemporary China,1 but they have overlooked that beneath the surface of a deceptively simple plot, what is truly Asian is more than just human behavior or traces of China's efforts at modernizing the Three Gorges. Beneath the protagonist Zhao's actions lies the traditional belief and customary practice of burying the dead in one's hometown so that the soul may rest in peace. Home is where one's roots are and hence constitutes what the rich finality of life means for a Chinese person, without which there is no consummation of life.

Getting home (c) 2007 by Ye Xiao Yi

Fig. 1: Film still, *Getting Home* (Zhang Yang, 2008).

(Not) The End: From Death to Life in East Asian Films

Zhao has the audacity and determination to transport his buddy Liu's body from Shenzhen to Chongqing (about 1,390 kilometers), for a proper burial (fig. 1). During his quest, the penniless Zhao encounters bullies, swindlers, and some kind souls who make his journey through isolated peaks and valleys bearable. I will first unpack what the Chinese title of the film alludes to and then highlight a scene in which Zhao participates as a paid mourner in a stranger's funeral wake.

2.1 A Ritual of Return

The original Chinese title of this film, *luo ye gui gen*, is a frequently recurring idiom on screen and in daily life, meaning "falling leaves return to their roots." This expression refers to how decomposed leaves return to earth, thus illustrating the state of overseas Chinese "as sojourners imbued with an irresistible urge to return"[2] to their birthplace, either alive or for burial. Among older generations of Chinese, at the end of life, the desire to die and be buried alongside their ancestors in the soil of home is particularly strong. Therefore, Zhao's unwavering decision to bring Liu's corpse back home is not merely fulfilling a promise to a friend or adhering to cultural norms; it honors an unspoken ritual of immense significance that embodies the sacredness of life.

Although the director may not have intentionally included elements of traditional religious practices, the transportation of a dead body is not without religious roots. In Hunan province, southern China, the folk practice of *gan shi* or "herding corpse," in which a Taoist priest leads a line of corpses to be transported back to their homeland, dates back to 1000 BCE.[3] Relevant for our discussion are not the technical aspects of how corpses were transported in ancient China, but that Zhao's insistence on his deceased friend's "going home" to rest in his home soil is an act grounded in cultural norms and rooted in religious traditions.

2.2 A Funeral Rehearsal and Memoir

Holding funeral wakes at home is a common practice among Chinese families, but rehearsing one's own death to the point of lying in a coffin is considered a taboo. In *Getting Home*, Zhao comes across a rich but lonely nameless elderly man who, with great fanfare, holds a rehearsal for his own funeral wake so that he can preside over it. He hires a huge entourage of mourners to perform the common customary practice of *ku sang*, literally, "funeral cry"), lamenting for him. As paid wailers,[4] the efficacy of their performance depends on how convincingly they act as the deceased's children and family members, which explains why high visibility and loud crying are required. When the man explains the rationale of his decision to Zhao, several medium close-up shots of his facial expressions reveal his uninhibited feelings of detachment and calmness, but with a tinge of melancholy. He philosophizes that since he has no descendants to conduct a wake for him after his death, he does it himself so that he can witness and experience the proceedings. Such anticipation of and preparation for death renders his existence greater authenticity, for it is a beautiful meditation on life.

Other funeral-themed movies include *Get Low* (Aaron Schneider, 2009), in which the protagonist hosts his own funeral party, and the cult classic *Harold and Maude* (Hal Ashby, 1971), featuring a death-obsessed teenage boy who attends a series of funerals to discover the meaning of life. What makes the funeral scene in *Getting Home* stand out from these western films is how the elderly man emphasizes the fact he has no posterity to attend to his funeral – Chinese children are expected to care for their parents until they breathe their last. Thus, this film undergirds a Confucian notion of filial piety and the obligations embedded in family relationships.[5]

The end of life will always raise complications and even mystical speculation about the afterlife. Yet the nameless elderly man's actions suggest that at its end, life is more than seeking closure. The transition to death marks how the deceased is etched into the memory of the living, and then, how the witnesses become harbingers of a collective memory of deceased persons. Only when discourses of memory cease, does a human being truly vanish from this world. Thus, a person persists beyond death through the memories of the living.

Viewed from this perspective, the funeral rehearsal is a microcosm of death, death rituals and memory that are within one's power to perform while one is still alive. The film's audience will notice the elaborate funeral objects and symbols and the exaggerated wailing of the professional mourners. The evocative appeal in anticipation of an afterlife as a worshiped ancestor – hence, being remembered – rather than being a wandering ghost cannot be overemphasized. Here, a living being is looking upon his own funerary process and witnessing his own altar set up; this is a formation of biographic memory and a way of putting his household and life in order.

The film's ending shows the landscape of Liu's hometown under urban reconstruction; all families have left. This seems to render Zhao's efforts in returning his friend's body futile, until he finds a note from Liu's son. Later, the police discover and cremate Liu's corpse, and the reliable Zhao is likely to embark on another expedition to return the ashes of the father to the son, thus perpetuating the notion of "return."

3. Balloon

Tibetan filmmaker Pema Tseden's *Balloon* focuses on pastoral Tibetan families born and raised in Tibet. This film opens with a breath-taking scene of Tibet's mountain plateaus as the protagonist, Dargye, is talking to his father. This is interrupted by Dargye's high-spirited but ignorant young sons playing with inflated translucent condoms, symbolizing birth control, stolen from under their parents' pillow, as if they were balloons. Several scenes later, we are told that Dargye's wife, Drolkar, is pregnant with their fourth child. In the film's social context of early-1980s China, the government just imposed a draconian one-child policy and failing to comply could mean losing their farm.

Midway through the film, Dargye's father passes away. Drolkar is willing to have an abortion, but Dargye opposes this vehemently for religious reasons: according to Tibetan Buddhist belief, the souls of ancestors reincarnate in unborn family members and relatives. Thus, the film presents the possibility that Dargye's father will be reborn as the child that Drolkar is carrying, an expectation that is highlighted in two important dreamlike scenes that underpin plot development.

3.1 Grandson: The Body as a Carrier of the Soul

The first "dream scene" follows a family dinner where the conversation centers on giving alms and renovating a temple, two acts of merit which Dargye's father, or Grandpa, greatly encourages. As they arrange to pray and donate to the offertory box[6] the following day, their focus shifts to a huge mole on the back of Jamyang, Dargye's oldest teenage son. They identify the mole as a confirmation of their grandmother's reincarnation: their belief that the body is only a "vehicle for the operation of consciousness, which alone encounters the signs of dying, rebirth and spiritual union"[7] is reaffirmed in her soul's occupation of Jamyang's body.

Between the scenes of family conversation and prayer in the temple full of lit candles is inserted an enigmatic bath scene. In a dimly lit bathroom we see the three boys, rubbing the back of their grandfather, discussing the latter's desire to be reborn as a family member. As one brother touches Jamyang's mole, the ceiling light begins to flicker. What happens next is utterly unexpected and unreal: one of the younger brothers removes Jamyang's huge mole from his back. Within seconds of fade-in and fade-out, the background changes to a vast desert plain, where the two naked brothers, laughing, sprint away with the mole while Jamyang, now fully clothed as if prepared for a journey, chases them. In this affective space, the emblematic mole is detached from his back, yet removing the mole in real life would have been impossible. Could this scene hint at Jamyang's inner desire to be freed from being the body receptacle of his grandmother's soul and from his family's traditions and customs, a desire that reflects his longing to shape his own destiny?

Further extending this interpretation, the continued spiritual existence of his grandmother is a parasite on Jamyang. Logically, this scene functions as a liminal space that allows Jamyang to move away from his ancestor's parasite-like existence, and on a larger scale, away from the reality and vicissitudes of the real world and ultimately from his obligations as the oldest grandson. Having been raised to adhere to religious traditions that emphasize family obligations, this is the only route of escape – an inconceivable, imaginative space – that allows Jamyang to navigate his ongoing struggle, which perhaps is unknown even to himself. This dream is both mirror and lamp, highlighting and reflecting the deep-rooted religious belief of death and rebirth.

The audience is not given any ebulliently melodramatic narrative but is compelled to perceive the unchangeable reality in which Jamyang has been raised and conditioned: at death, human consciousness perishes only to be reborn to a subsequent consciousness. This explains why the family members' grief over Grandpa's death seems short-lived because ascertaining where his soul migrates is their chief concern.

3.2 Grandfather: The Soul in Need of a Body

As arguments take place regarding Drolkar's decision to terminate her pregnancy, Grandpa dies. It logically follows that the grandfather's possibility of rebirth hinges solely on Drolkar keeping the fetus. Drolkar's sister, the nun Shangchu Drolma, provides additional insight regarding the grievous implications of abortion in her attempt to persuade Drolkar to keep the baby.

Abortion has always been a controversial issue. Non-Tibetans may deem it as an ethical, moral and legal issue, but through Shangchu Drolma's explanation to her sister, director Pema Tseden represents it as a religious issue, a sin. Since a deceased person has already worked for the "accumulated merit" that is required for rebirth, if the selected living body refuses to cooperate, the soul attempting to return would suffer eternally. Shangchu Drolma refers to her own past "irredeemable sins," hinting that she is paying restitution as a nun for a past abortion. The nun urges her sister to believe the Buddhist lama, who confirmed that Grandpa is in the process of rebirth. Repudiating the lama's instructions and denying Grandpa's rebirth as her baby would also be a sin.

A second illusory scene follows the sisters' dialogue. Shortly after Grandpa's death, Jamyang enters a surreal cosmic landscape repeatedly crying out, "Grandpa, Grandpa." The camera pans slowly, showing a vertically inverted screen with the top one-third of the frame as a boundless transcendent realm along which the reverse silhouette of a man glides holding a *mala* (prayer beads) in his hands (fig. 2). The rest of the frame is filled with a cloud-like, massive dark-colored puddle.[8] In between the frames, striking amber light shines through. Pema Tseden adopts this unconventional but visually stunning upside-down frame to convey the ethereal moments during which rebirth into a new body is said to occur. This cinematographic technique helps viewers to visualize the invisible, indescribable realms, reminiscent of Terrence Malick's provocative scenes of biblical creation in his 2011 epic, *The Tree of Life*.

Balloons (c) 2019 by Ye Xiao Yi

Fig. 2: Film still, *Balloon* (Pema Tseden 2019).

There is a sense in which the destiny and existence of mother and baby are defined by the religious understanding of rebirth and reincarnation in Tibetan Buddhist cosmology.[9] Concerns of pregnancy, financial challenges, death in the family, and modernity versus traditions are but narratives interwoven into a layered story. Threading through these events is the perennial theme of rebirth and reincarnation. The overarching storyline may present a couple who keeps producing babies due to the husband's unchecked libido, but in the context of Tibetan nomadic pastoralism, more sons mean having the manpower needed to herd the sheep. The state birth control policies and the shortage of condoms in the clinics may threaten their livelihood, but the crux of the matter embedded within this socio-political issue is really the mysterious meaning of death and the endless continuation of life.

4. Conclusion

Getting Home and *Balloon* describe the diverse manifestations of the life-death paradox where the characters' courage, fear and resilience find expression in Chinese and Tibetan religious traditions. Although each tradition has its distinctive way of engaging the complexities of life and

(Not) The End: From Death to Life in East Asian Films

death, we find the dignity and evanescence of life reaffirmed in both. At least two common aspects are identifiable in these films. First, the seemingly mundane practice of laying the dead at rest in their hometown is deeply spiritual and ritualistic in nature. As such, we observe the sacred in the everyday as reflected in the actions of the living. Religious ceremonies, even if they mean breaking the taboo of holding one's own funeral, accentuate the significance of a proper burial and the human longing to be remembered. Second, death represents a new journey for both the living person who attends to the affairs of the dead (Zhao's trek) and the deceased (rebirth). But life, death and the continuity of life are also interlaced with distinct meanings for the characters: in *Getting Home* Zhao demonstrates how one can live for a deceased friend, while the deceased grandfather in *Balloon* contrives to live through an unborn child.

Notes

1. See, for instance, Derek Elley, "Getting Home," Variety, 12 March 2007, at https://variety.com/2007/film/markets-festivals/getting-home-1200509755/ [9 January 2021].
2. L. Ling-chi Wang, "Roots and the Changing Identity of the Chinese in the United States," in Tu Wei-ming (ed.), *The Living Tree: The Changing Meaning of Being Chinese Today*, Stanford: Stanford University Press, 1994, 185–212, here 187.
3. Zhu Weijin, "The Real Walking Dead: A Look Behind the Ancient Chinese Tradition of Corpse Walking," *The World of Chinese*, at https://www.theworldofchinese.com/2014/05/the-real-walking-dead/ [23 January 2021]. See also Zhang Da-wei, "On the Religious and Ethical Implications of Ganshi in Xiangxi: Concurrently Discuss Primitive Belief as a Way of Human Existence," Journal of Qiannan Normal University for Nationalities 36.4 (2016), 18–22.
4. There are similar performative elements in laments by Bangladeshi, Egyptian, Irish, and Jewish wailers, some of whom are hired. See James M. Wilce's seminal work, *Crying Shame: Metaculture, Modernity, and the Exaggerated Death of Lament*, New York: Wiley, 2008.
5. See case studies of how deeply Confucian values and Chinese religions influence Chinese patients under palliative care in Harold Coward/Elizabeth Causton, "'A Good Death' in Hospice Palliative Care," in Christopher M. Moreman (ed.), *The Routledge Companion to Death and Dying*, London: Taylor & Francis, 2018, 442–454, here 449–450.
6. At the temple, they will *tian xiang* you (literally, "add oil to the lamps"). This generic term describes a worship practice whereby believers donate money to buy oil to keep the altar lamps burning. The money in the offertory box can be used for other purposes relating to the temple and matters of worship.
7. Raymond L. M. Lee, "Eternity Calling: Modernity and the Revival of Death and the Afterlife," in Helaine Selin/Robert¬ M.¬ Rako (eds.), *Death Across Cultures: Death and Dying in Non-Western Cultures*, Cham: Springer, 2019, 335–349, here 377.
8. Mountains and lakes are common sacred sites in Tibetan spirituality. For the silhouette to move within an environment of water puddle bears a profound message that it is the soul of a dead person since it is inverted, hence, abnormal.

9. Even in pre-Buddhist times, a belief in some form of rebirth existed in Tibet. With the arrival of Buddhism in the seventh century, reincarnation became one of the main tenets of the Tibetan worldview. As a Tibetan Buddhist ethical and metaphysical principle, a person's endless rebirth into cyclic existences (or *saṃsāra*) is dependent upon deeds and morality. Later, Tibetans expanded the basic structure of Mahāyāna (Great Vehicle) Buddhism. See, for instance, Matthew Kapstein, *The Tibetan Assimilation of Buddhism: Conversion, Contestation, and Memory*, Oxford: Oxford University Press, 2000, 38–50.

Health Care Practice at the End of Life: Addressing Opposite Attitudes and Diverse Contexts

ANDREA VICINI

Context influences how people live and die, and the availability of health care. Moreover, attitudes define how care is offered and how death is experienced. In the Global North, technological developments assure a better quality of life, but death is experienced as an enemy to fight and defeat in hospitals, often alone. In the Global South, with communal support, death is the ultimate dimension of human existence. Contexts and attitudes inform people's agency. Hence, the ethical responses vary: from resisting the medicalization of death to systemic and structural changes. Virtuous behaviors are possible; some are inspired by poems and the spiritual tradition.

For some people, death is the ultimate enemy to defeat. Death challenges and haunts each one and, particularly, health care professionals. For others, death is integral to being human, the sole certainty in life, and what waits at the end of one's life journey. These two ways of experiencing death might prevail in different stages of one's life and exemplify how people can experience their dying in diverse contexts.

In developed countries, inequities continue to be present – whether in the case of race, age, gender, class, nationality, and economic status – and influence one's life and death. In health care settings, relying on all medical resources available is the dominating approach, causing high expenses at the end of life. In these contexts, despite skilled palliative care, when death is approaching, letting go is counter-cultural. The promises of technological fixes, procedures, and new experimental drugs are seductive, both for patients and health care professionals. Medical technology seems to offer ways to avoid considering death as what ends our existence.

In medical circles, the dominant rhetoric focuses on attackers and invaders – bacteria, parasites, viruses, cancer cells, even one's own cells as in autoimmune diseases. Hence, health care professionals wage wars against pervasive and subtle enemies. The risk is that animosity against these aggressors might lead to blindness regarding what happens to patients, whose fragility and vulnerability is lost and hurt by such war rhetoric. The sick become casualties in wars they did not wage. In the past, one metaphysical poem expressed this pathologic dynamic, and pointed to an alternative approach.

1. Death as an Enemy, or as a Pause
In 1999, the American playwright Margaret Edson won the Pulitzer Prize in drama with her play *Wit*, which, in 2001, became a television movie directed by Mike Nichols, with Emma Thompson as the leading character, Vivian Bering. The career of Professor Vivian Bearing, an expert in the 17th-century British poet John Donne (1572–1631), was shaped by her literary competence on matters of death. Diagnosed with advanced ovarian cancer, her physician encouraged her to undergo an experimental and aggressive chemotherapy, which was unsuccessful and progressively worsened her quality of life. However, the research needs had to prevail over the patient's well-being and the clinical trial continued. Both cancer and death were enemies to be defeated.

Revisiting a turning point in her career, Vivian appreciated what her mentor stressed in interpreting the final line of Donne's sonnet 'Death be not proud' (1610). The sonnet begins with the account of the struggle to vanquish death as the enemy. The ending, however, differs according to the translator's choice regarding the final verse's punctuation. As a student writing on the poem, Vivian had chosen a common, melodramatic translation. As a result, the poem described the ultimate encounter with death as performing a drama on a stage, with death gloriously defeated: 'And Death shall be no more; Death, thou shalt die!'

Disappointed by such a choice, Vivian's mentor pointed to the critical edition of the English literary critic Helen Gardner (1908–1986), who, in the last verse, placed a comma – a pause – instead of a semicolon – a stronger separation. Hence, in Gardner's rendering, the final verse reads: 'And death shall be no more, death thou shalt die.'[1] As both the play and the movie stress, in that simple choice, truthful to the metaphysical poem, stands the difference between fighting against death, standing proud in front of it, while experiencing death as an invincible and powerful enemy, or accepting death. Death is like a comma – a pause – placed between the life we know now, and the gift of a never-ending life prepared for us. Just a comma separates finitude from eternity. Life and death are not insuperable barriers, they are just like a comma.

Death as a pause is a simple truth, at least for Christian faith and because of inner freedom. However, if generalizations are allowed, in developed countries we might have lost the ability of experiencing death as a pause, as a simple comma in the whole sentence of our existence.

Just as described in *Wit*, in the Global North, where health care is fully developed and displays technological prowess, professionals might be tempted to stand proud in facing death, even when patients and common sense suggest that continuing treatments at any cost does not mean caring for the patients' well-being. Death is medicalized and transformed into a clinical occurrence instead of approaching it as a human reality.

Whether at home or in dedicated facilities, palliative care and hospice care avoid the ferocity of medical treatments at the end of one's life. Such care provides expert accompaniment and support, fostering people's quality of life. The dying are helped to breathe easily, avoid or contain pain, and protect their limited mobility. In many cases, these sick stay at their homes, surrounded by their memories and relationships. Hence, patients are the center of care. Eventually, the dying person will face death, but as what pauses their lives. Death is not the enemy – just everyone's ultimate encounter.

The distinction between overzealous treatments and letting go at the end of one's life is explicit in some health care literature[2] and, in the Catholic context, in magisterial documents, including the recent letter of the Congregation for the Doctrine of the Faith (CDF), *Samaritanus Bonus: On the Care of Persons in the Critical and Terminal Phases of Life and the New Charter for Health Care Workers.*[3] The Charter stresses that, "A sick person in the terminal stage of his [sic] illness should receive all forms of care that allow for alleviation of the painfulness of the dying process" (no. 147), even in the case of "deep palliative sedation in the terminal stage, when clinically motivated" (no. 155). In its Letter, the CDF is concerned about possible abuses (i.e. euthanasia) and argues that it "is desirable to extend palliative treatments to those who need them, within the limits of what is fiscally possible, and to assist them in the terminal stages of life, but as an integrated approach to the care of existing chronic or degenerative pathologies involving a complex prognosis that is unfavorable and painful for the patient and family" (part V, no. 4).

2. From the Margins

In both documents, however, one finds a surprising omission: no attention is given to the diverse contexts across the globe where people live and end their lives. To die in New York is not comparable to live and end one's life in slums, bidonvilles, refugee camps, or isolated villages. On these margins, daily and without interruption, people face incredible challenges. Health care facilities might be absent, distant, or offering limited services. Prevention is a mirage. Diagnosis is expensive. Treatments are not affordable. Military conflicts and social unrest threaten care and ordinary life.

In these troubled contexts, people risk being harmed, abused, and violated – e.g., in the case of women – or seized and forced to become child soldiers or adolescent killers. Death is not aseptic, as in clinics and hospitals in the Global North. Death is dirty, messy, as a relentless presence. Moreover, in many locations in the Global South, people's death is out in the open and not segregated in clinical settings; it occurs mostly at home, and health care systems are unable to medicalize death.

To reflect on the end of life in the Global South means to critically examine the conditions that do not allow personal and social flourishing. Hence, while strengthening health care systems is an urgent priority, one should also consider the social and political determinants of health, i.e., all the factors that influence one's quality of life: from access to healthy, nutritious food and clean water to sanitation and safe roads; from education to political participation; from safe and justly retributed jobs to non-polluted environments. To recognize how people die in these contexts requires a commitment to promote social justice and people's quality of life.

Health is a common, global good. Everyone benefits from healthier ways of living, better primary care, and health services available and accessible to all. The training of health care workers should imply attractive opportunities for serving the local population by practicing in one's own country. The "pull" effect of countries in the Global North, which need caretakers, nurses, and physicians trained in the Global South to satisfy their needs of skilled personnel, is a systemic dynamic that should be resisted. At the same time, the "push" effect, which forces professionals to migrate in order to work in better conditions, requires structural transformations to create opportunities in one's own country.

While avoiding oversimplifications, in the Global South it is easier to encounter more communal contexts, where deliberation and even consent include some level of communal engagement. In the African continent, the palaver ethics exemplifies a shared and interactive space for reflection, debate, and deliberation.[4] Without cheap idealizations, and well aware that communities can stigmatize, marginalize, and ostracize the vulnerable leading to exclusion and social "death," communities can foster positive interactions and accompany people at the end of their lives in caring ways. Striving for meaningful communal interactions expresses a need for conversion in social contexts dominated by individualistic attitudes and behaviors.

For Christianity, all human beings are created in the image of God, share the same dignity and deserve compassionate and competent care. Hence, ethical analysis critically assesses inequities that influence people's lives and their deaths. Context is relevant. As history teaches us, wealth and privilege, which mostly characterize the Global North, depend, in large part, on the colonial exploitation of many countries in the Global South and on continuing powerful dynamics that, internationally, limit social and political development, including health care. Hence, global public health contributes to examine and address everything that influences the experience of death today.

3. Global Public Health
The global pandemic caused by COVID-19 has tragically led the world

to experience death in dramatic ways. In each country, the daily bulletins count who was infected and died, and evoke the stories of each one of those persons and of those mourning them. Because of the gravity of their health conditions and of the strict restrictions imposed to contain spreading the infection, isolation and loneliness characterized those deaths. The only accompaniment was assured by grieving health care professionals, overburdened by the sheer magnitude of the pandemic in overwhelmed health care settings.

In the Global North, the scale of the pandemic and the great loss of human lives – particularly of the elderly – stressed the vulnerability and fragility of health care systems, despite the technological prowess of the services provided and the outstanding quality of care that is offered. Moreover, COVID-19 highlighted and worsened the disparities and inequities that characterize health care systems and delivery, as well as the quality of life on the planet and within countries. In rich countries, racial and ethnic minorities, indigenous communities, the elderly, immigrants, undocumented people, prisoners, the homeless, and those who belong to the low-income population suffered greatly and disproportionately.

As the physician and anthropologist Paul Farmer stresses, diseases have a preferential option for the poor and they require fostering a "pragmatic solidarity," striving to promote social justice and liberation from any oppressive dynamic and structure.[5] By embracing the critical analysis and ethical agenda of liberation theology, and the richness of Catholic social thought and action, Farmer invites us to *see* how people get sick, suffer, and die; *judge* situations and institutions by assessing how just or unjust they are; and *act* to promote the common good with a particular attention to who is marginalized, excluded, and discriminated. Moreover, action is neither paternalistic nor patronizing. On the contrary, in order to promote social justice, we act together, in solidarity, joining those who are oppressed, abandoned, forgotten, and excluded. The coronavirus global pandemic calls us to embrace pragmatic solidarity and realize systemic and structural reforms that enable greater justice in our world.

The vaccination process is an opportunity for a just response, by vaccinating everyone, everywhere. However, the COVID-19 pandemic showed again how countries and people are valued differently, even in the case of what affects the whole humankind. Vaccinations are privileging the richer nations. If the vaccination pace in the Global South will not improve, it might take years to vaccinate the populations in low-income countries. Surprisingly, the developed nations seem to forget that viruses do not respect barriers. The pandemic will end when the majority of the world population will be vaccinated, reaching the needed global herd immunity. Self-interest is not the best ethical motivator, but it should contribute to generate a stronger commitment to promote health, protect lives, and avoid further compromising fragile economies in our interconnected world. The determination and commitment of non-profit organizations (e.g., COVAX, and the Bill and Melinda Gates Foundation) to bolster the vaccination process in the Global South are reassuring and encouraging.

Moreover, in developing countries, the global pandemic further challenged people living in social contexts often shaken by conflicts and political instability, and burdened by insufficient economic development. COVID-19 added its burden to the other pre-existing pandemic diseases that already affect many nations – i.e., HIV/AIDS, malaria, and tuberculosis – with their toll on people's quality of life, economic production, and loss of human lives.

4. To Change and to Transform

To reflect on the end of life does not imply to assume that, in many situations, death is ineluctable and unavoidable. Learning to let go, in specific situations at the end of our lives, requires to avoid choosing overzealous treatments. Opting for these treatments seems to depend on the difficulty to accept our finitude and dying, and on the relatively easy access to technologically advanced health care services. At the same time, striving for promoting human dignity, social justice, and a quality of life worthy of human beings is morally necessary.

To realize that our lives end should neither lead to disengagement nor resignation. Injustice is humanly unacceptable. Inequities should not be tolerated. Change and transformation should foster greater social equality. Hence, any reflection on people's end of life should be accompanied by considering what concerns one's quality of life and the existing conditions which depend on social arrangements – i.e., the quality, presence, and availability of health care services for all, particularly those in greater need and with more limited financial resources.

Where and how people live matters. If the social context does not allow citizens to flourish, as a society we are responsible for what shortens people's lives and causes their death. Together with disease and pandemics, the dire consequences of climate change threaten the lives of many people by increasing personal and social vulnerability, particularly in the Global South. Moreover, the presence of ambient and environmental pollution requires urgent interventions aimed at reducing and eliminating them.

A consistent ethic of life, proposed by the late cardinal of Chicago, Joseph Bernardin (1928–1996), allows us to articulate a comprehensive ethical approach that engages all dimensions of human life.[6] Then, the ethical agenda will set priorities by considering who is in greater need, where, and which help should be provided.

A systemic approach which encompasses a critical analysis of social structures, is integral to reflections on health. With its wisdom tested by time, the spiritual tradition further enriches transformative dynamics by stressing how change is multilayered and engages both individuals and communities.

5. Learning from the Past

Spiritual discourse described death as our sister, not as an enemy. In his Canticle of the Creatures, Francis of Assisi (1181/1182–1226) dared to sing, "Be praised my Lord, for our Sister, Bodily Death, from whom no man living can escape."[7]

One could dismiss Francis's experience as isolated, elitist, and the fruit of his spiritual journey. However, Christianity promoted collective opportunities for spiritual growth, often in liturgical and para-liturgical forms. As an example, in many places Good Friday processions and dramatizations allow many to avoid being disengaged bystanders and facilitate people's participation, joining in reenacting Jesus's death as a communal event that touches all the senses and, hopefully, nourishes the spiritual life, individually and communally. Believers do not avoid the tragedy of Jesus's death, but, in limited and faulty ways, are present to Jesus's drama and ordeal – at least liturgically and in prayer.

These dramatizations do not manifest a macabre taste. Within theological discourse, Christopher Vogt revisits the Gospel narrative of Jesus's passion and death by stressing how it informs our understanding of Jesus's dying and could influence how Christians end their lives. For Vogt, Luke's Gospel stresses patience, compassion, and hope.[8] Jesus's virtuous ways empower his disciples to become virtuous – even in dying. Throughout the history of Christianity, virtues shaped how people cared for the sick and dying, how they died, and they could continue to inform how health care is provided and how one's dies. Many longed for a quick end with a good and peaceful death, surrounded by caring and loving people, or departing while asleep. For others, the ineluctability of death was mitigated by the possibility of preparing for it, together with others, cultivating the *ars moriendi*.

As the term *ars* indicates, such preparation neither expressed a sick attraction for death, nor exorcised death.[9] On the contrary, together, people fostered virtuous attitudes and strengthened their freedom, preparing themselves to face their death. The communal support provided by confraternities helped to avoid experiencing death as a looming reality that negatively affects one's well-being and flourishing. Death was not an impending doom. As Paul wrote, echoing the prophet Hosea: "Where, O death, is your sting?" (1 Cor 15:55; Hos 13:14; NRSV). Preparing for death with others nourished a strong sense of communal support in ordinary life. Death was experienced as the turning point that would further expand the experience of earthly community with the communion of saints and divine intimacy.

Theologically, the *ars moriendi* is an incarnational process. Jesus's life and death manifest the divine incarnated and allow believers to experience being created in the image of God, blessed with the gift of joining God's work, and made for eternal life in God. Moreover, the communal dimension was not limited to belonging to confraternities and to participating in their activities. Virtuous practices were integral components of the ars moriendi. Among the corporal works of mercy, caring for the sick and the dying had special relevance. At the same time, a Pelagian approach was lingering, subtly or explicitly (e.g., in the case of the indulgences), implying that believers had to earn their place in eternal life. Among other transformative contributions that challenged these rationales, the Protestant Reformations promoted a historic purification of a problematic understanding of human agency regarding one's life, death, and the gift of life everlasting. Salvation is neither merited nor earned. The uncertainty of death, and the impossibility of controlling one's redemption and the gift of the resurrection, should not transform caring for people in need, and particularly the dying, in a passport to secure a sure passage to the afterlife.

Without nostalgia for bygone times, the *ars moriendi* exemplifies the possibility of dealing virtuously with the certainty of one's dying and death. Moreover, with due adaptations, because of their anthropological, relational, and spiritual dimensions, even today these practices could shape personal and social dynamics.[10] Finally, communal forms of accompaniment, inspired by a revisited *ars moriendi*, could influence how death is experienced in health care contexts, by patients and family members, professionals, chaplains, and pastoral ministers.

6. Conclusion

Diverse virtues inform how people live and die. At the end of our lives, efforts to reconcile with loved ones and friends might lead to a greater inner freedom and even some form of peace, learning to let go, avoiding overzealous treatments, and approaching death accompanied by the consoling presence of a reconciled heart and the proximity of family members, relatives, friends, and caring professionals.

However, how we live and die depends also on health care contexts. Globally, health care institutions should strive to be virtuous, too, in diverse ways: from resisting excessive medicalization in the Global North to addressing systemic and structural inequities in the Global South. Hence, how people end their lives and how health care is provided could foster a consistent and comprehensive ethic of life.

Notes

1. John Donne, *The Elegies, and the Songs and Sonnets,* translated by Helen Gardner, Oxford: Clarendon Press, 1965.
2. Atul Gawande, *Being Mortal: Medicine and What Matters in the End*, New York: Metropolitan Books, 2014.
3. Congregation for the Doctrine of the Faith, "Samaritanus Bonus: On the Care of Persons in the Critical and Terminal Phases of Life," 14 July 2020, https://www.vatican.va/roman_curia/congregations/cfaith/documents/rc_con_cfaith_doc_20200714_samaritanus-bonus_en.html#_ftnref64; *Pontifical Council for Pastoral Assistance to Health Care Workers, New Charter for Health Care Workers*, Philadelphia: National Catholic Bioethics Center, 2017, nos. 58, 85, 93, 147, 155.

4. Bénézet Bujo, *Foundations for an African Ethics: Beyond the Universal Claims of Western Morality*, Nairobi: Paulines, 2003, 67–97; Laurenti Magesa, *Anatomy of Inculturation: Transforming the Church in Africa*, Nairobi: Paulines, 2004, 177–180; Anna Floerke Scheid, "Under the Palaver Tree: Community Ethics for Truth-telling and Reconciliation," *Journal of the Society of Christian Ethics* 31.1 (2011), 17–36.

5. Paul Farmer, *Pathologies of Power: Health, Human Rights*, and the New War on the Poor, Berkeley: University of California Press, 2005, 220.

6. Thomas A. Nairn (ed.), *The Consistent Ethic of Life: Assessing Its Reception and Relevance*, Maryknoll: Orbis Books, 2008; Joseph Bernardin, The Seamless Garment: Writings on the Consistent Ethic of Life, Maryknoll: Orbis Books, 2008.

7. Roger D. Sorrell, *St. Francis of Assisi and Nature: Tradition and Innovation in Western Christian Attitudes toward the Environment*, New York: Oxford University Press, 1988, 101; see also 98.

8. Christopher P. Vogt, "Practicing Patience, Compassion, and Hope at the End of Life: Mining the Passion of Jesus in 'Luke' for a Christian Model of Dying Well," *Journal of the Society of Christian Ethics* 24.1 (2004), 135–158; Christopher P. Vogt, *Patience, Compassion, Hope, and the Christian Art of Dying Well*, Lanham: Rowman & Littlefield, 2004.

9. Vogt, *Patience, Compassion, Hope*; Allen Verhey, The Christian Art of Dying: Learning from Jesus, Grand Rapids: William B. Eerdmans, 2011; Joseph E. Davis/ Paul Joseph Scherz (eds.), *The Evening of Life: The Challenges of Aging and Dying Well*, Notre Dame: University of Notre Dame Press, 2020.

10. Kerry S. Walters, *The Art of Dying and Living: Lessons Form Saints of Our Time*, Maryknoll: Orbis Books, 2011.

The End of Life in a Global Health Perspective

ALEXANDRE A. MARTINS

With the development of modern medicine and the possibility of increasing human longevity, people's attitudes toward their end of life have changed. However, the benefits of modern medicine have not been available to all. Consequently, many people have been more vulnerable to illnesses and even suffered premature death despite our current medical development. This paper focuses on end-of-life experiences in contexts marked by poverty and oppression. It engages narratives of unjust deaths as a result of social vulnerability and lack of health care to challenge the ways that end-of-life issues are considered in global health. Following Pope Francis's invitation to listen and learn from those at the bottom of society, this paper examines end-of-life challenges in global health in dialogue with marginalized people.

This essay is grounded on a theological approach that comes from below, that is, from the experience of the people at the bottom of societies. The poor are the people who best represent this bottom. I present their narratives as the starting point, or theological locus, to address the end of life in a global health perspective. The shift from a view that begins at the top – represented by theoretical approaches or by looking at problems that impact rich nations – to a perspective from below, significantly impacts the way we do theological bioethics and see end-of-life challenges. To illustrate this shift, I present a short anecdote that highlights this reality.

In September of 2020, I was part of a panel on death and COVID-19 at a health care ethics conference in the USA. My presentation highlighted the situation of indigenous people in the Amazon region in Brazil who were getting infected and dying isolated without access to medical care. The other panelists presented ethical issues in the USA about people dying in ICUs without seeing a family member, with no spiritual care, the possibility of rationing ICUs, and questions regarding CPR and DNR. All these issues were relevant, and the audience engaged with the panelists with questions and comments. The discussion moved to euthanasia, medical futility, and death with dignity in the USA, focused on the physician-patient relationship, particularly in this pandemic. Immediately they began to address end-of-life controversies related to biomedical ethics. My talk about indigenous deaths because of their disproportionate vulnerability and lack of access to minimal health care was lost in the conversation, until, close to the end, the convener asked what I thought about the discussion. My answer was very simple: you are only talking about challenges that impact those who have access to health care, with the privilege to choose between CPR or DNR, and to refuse care at the end of life if they want. In the reality of the poor where I serve, most people do not have a chance to see a physician or a nurse. Many of those who see a health care professional find a person overwhelmed with their work and the lack of adequate resources to serve the sick.

In the reality of the poor and the oppressed, the biggest challenge for the end of life is not the ability to choose or refuse certain medical services, but rather it is dying prematurely without proper care or access to medical assistance. Most people do not arrive at this stage of care with the privilege to choose or refuse specific treatments. Rather, poverty and structures of oppression that perpetuate injustice and marginalization make people vulnerable to diseases, deny them health care, and condemn them to premature death.[1]

1. The Suffering of the Poor and Their Premature Deaths: A Scandal of Injustice in Global Health

Many studies show that poverty, oppression, and injustice are the main causes of sickness and premature death in the world. These are social determinants of health. The poor disproportionally fall sick and die because of bio-socio-economic factors and lack of access to health care.[2] Although the statistics are shocking, we get used to them and do not see the faces and the stories behind them. This is also the case with the COVID-19 pandemic. People suffering and dying are not merely statistics. They are individuals, with their stories and dignity. Theologically speaking, they are crucified people whose faces we are invited to contemplate as we contemplate the face of Jesus on the cross. Jesus identifies himself with the suffering of the poor.

I present two stories that illustrate this reality of injustice and death, and which at the same time capture the individual lives to be contemplated. José Manuel da Silva, a 20-year-old, died in the emergency room (ER) at Hospital Ipiranga, after being shot by police officers who thought he was part of a gang of drug traffickers of a favela in São Paulo, Brazil. I don't know the details of this persecution and killing, and why José was targeted. But I know that it was later proved that he was not part of this gang. He never used drugs and worked in a supermarket. However, José was a black, poor guy who was mistakenly targeted by a police with a history of brutality and bias against African-Brazilians. The story of José illustrates many stories of black, poor and young people who are victims of police brutality and the structural violence of the criminal system.

My meeting with José was short and unforgettable. In the early 2000s, I was serving as a nursing student at the ER of Hospital Ipiranga, a public hospital near the favela where José lived. On a Thursday, at about 5pm, police officers arrived at the ER with two young boys who were shot by them. I was part of the team in charge of José, who had two shots in his chest, was unconscious, and went into cardiopulmonary arrest. We immediately began CPR. I was the person doing compressions. Police officers were yelling bad words at us that we couldn't allow this "criminal" to die. What was already a very tense situation in an overcrowded hospital, with many people waiting for assistance in the ER, became more stressful with the attitude of the officers. Unfortunately, we were not able to save José. He died. My team was speechless while a police officer said: "This son of a bitch is lucky, better die here than suffer in the hands of prisoners." I didn't know what to think. The physician, leading the team, asked a colleague and me to take care of the body and bring it to the morgue where a forensic doctor would examine the body. José was only three years younger than I. I couldn't see any evil on him, but I saw so much evil in the situation of the police officers yelling while we were trying to save him. Even if he was guilty, I thought he deserved better. I thought José had a mother and a family who loved him. He was not only a statistic of police killing, he was also one more statistic in a system of structural violence against black and poor people. A young innocent man who lost his life in a very undignified and unjust way. Poverty, racism, and violence killed one more person whose story, with its dreams of a better life, I never learned. But I knew they existed. José's face was once again the suffering face of Jesus in the cross, killed by a system of oppression, injustice, and violence.

The second story is about indigenous people in the Amazon region in Brazil and their suffering because of COVID-19. The indigenous people are perhaps those who have most experienced the devastations of their communities because of infectious diseases brought by outsiders. Since the arrival of the Portuguese in Brazil, infectious diseases brought by them, such as flu, smallpox, measles, chickenpox, tuberculosis, and STIs, were weapons used along with their guns to kill the indigenous in their own lands. It is estimated that Brazil had 1,422 different indigenous peoples, with 40 linguistic families and 33 isolated languages in the 1500s, with a population of 40 million. Today, these people are approximately 800,000, divided in 225 indigenous peoples, with 21 linguistic families. Most of these peoples are in the Amazon region.[3]

The COVID-19 pandemic is not a new story for indigenous people. Rather it is another cruel page in the story of historically oppressed original peoples. The bitter memories of previous epidemics have been reawakened by COVID-19. According to anthropologist Carlos Fausto, "since the beginning of colonization, [indigenous peoples] had to learn the meaning of 'epidemic' in their own bodies." Fausto reports the words of his friend from the Kuikuro people: "[COVID] is like the measles of my grandfather's time." (A reference to the deeply traumatic account of the measles epidemic in 1954.) "[The disease] was sudden and swift, killing entire families without even leaving time to bury the dead properly. With everyone sick, no one was left to provide food, much less tend to the bodies."[4]

Numbers from Brazilian Health Ministry's Special Secretary for Indigenous Health show that the COVID-19 mortality rate among indigenous is 52 per 100,000 while among the general non-indigenous

Brazilians, it is 21 per 100,000. Indigenous individuals living in urban areas are five times more likely to be infected by the coronavirus and need hospitalization than non-indigenous.[5] Ricardo Ventura Santos and colleagues affirm:

> "The crisis caused by the COVID-19 pandemic clearly exposes indigenous peoples' greater political, social, and environmental vulnerability. Experiencing daily violence and discrimination, indigenous people in Brazil live in precarious housing and sanitation conditions; face invaders and the damage caused to their territories; deal with food insecurity and lack of safe water, high infant mortality, invisibility of the indigenous families living in cities and towns; [and] childhood marked by chronic malnutrition." [6]

The original peoples of Brazil have suffered attacks against their lives by farmers and gold miners who invade their lands. They use armed militias to create a true war that has killed hundreds and displaced thousands of indigenous. These farmers deforest the Amazon rainforest for industrial agriculture and livestock, and gold miners devastate the forest searching for gold and other minerals. The administration of the current Brazilian president, Jair Bolsonaro, supports these actions against the forest and their peoples, and COVID-19 seems to be used as an opportunity to accelerate the elimination of the indigenous peoples. According to President Bolsonaro, they are lazy and unproductive people who prevent the country from development.[7]

Theologian Élio Gasda challenges this narrative and suggests that the Brazilian state is being dismantled by President Bolsonaro and that COVID-19 is being used to promote a genocide of the indigenous people.[8] Gasda stresses that the indigenous dying are not merely statistics, but people with names and stories. He highlights for example the Yanomami mothers who are losing their children from COVID-19 and are also denied the right to a funeral according to their traditions because the state is burying people in mass graves. The Yanomami do not bury their dead, but rather burn them in a communitarian ritual, an important ceremony of passage full of meaning.[9]

2. The End of Life of the Poor and the Oppressed in Global Health

These stories reveal that the most urgent global health challenges for the end of life in low- and middle-income countries (LMIC) are far from discussions about euthanasia and medical futility. When we look at the realities in which these people die and contemplate their faces, we realize the end of life in global health is challenged by the drama of injustice and premature death without dignity.

The development of modern medicine and the possibility of increasing human longevity and wellbeing are great achievements for humanity, but paradoxically they are also a failure because the majority of the world's population is excluded from this development. Indeed, many people have been more vulnerable and even suffered premature death despite our current medical progress. This fact challenges us to expand our theological bioethics reflection on end-of-life issues.

In recent documents, the Catholic teaching on the end of life has been limited to issues related to euthanasia, physician assisted suicide, and palliative care. The Church aims to provide resources for a death with dignity, without choosing its anticipation which the Magisterium considers a "grave violation of the law of God."[10] The latest document of the Congregation for the Doctrine of the Faith (CDF) on the end of life clearly condemns euthanasia as "a crime against human life because, in this act, one chooses directly to cause the death of another innocent human being."[11] Yet these documents illustrate that the Church's teaching on the end of life is limited to a first world discussion about patient autonomy and the use of medical technology to extend or abbreviate life.

The CDF's document provides a great pastoral theology for care at the end of life, using the Good Samaritan to stress the Church's mission of care for those who are dying. However, it does not address any issues related to death because of poverty and lack of health care. Evangelium vitae considers social injustice as threat for life:

> "Today this proclamation is especially pressing because of the extraordinary increase and gravity of threats to the life of individuals and peoples, especially where life is weak and defenseless. In addition to the ancient scourges of poverty, hunger, endemic diseases, violence and war, new threats are emerging on an alarmingly vast scale."[12]

However, John Paul II failed to relate these threats to health care systems and the lack of medical assistance, especially in the LMIC. When addressing end-of-life issues, he also limited himself to discussions of euthanasia, medical futility, and palliative care. Moreover, none of these documents includes the voices of people at the end of life, either from rich countries, or from the LMIC. Global health does not seem to be a concern and the discussion is narrowed to the physician-patient relationship.

However, Pope Francis's teaching provides a perspective that can advance the discussion about the end of life in ways that attend to the realities in the LMIC. Consistently, in his major writings, Francis stresses the importance of listening to the poor in a posture open to learn from them. In his first document, Francis suggested: "I prefer a Church which is bruised, hurting, and dirty because it has been out on the streets, rather than a Church which is unhealthy from being confined and from clinging to its own security."[13] This Church incarnates "the duty of hearing the cry of the poor"[14] to "learn from them."[15] Thus, we can "properly accompany the poor in their path of liberation."[16] In *Laudato si'*, Francis expanded this perspective by developing a theology of dialogical encounter with those who are at the bottom of society, in which he included the indigenous communities as "dialogical partners" from whom we have much to listen and learn.[17] The Synod of Bishops on the Amazon confirmed this view of encounter and dialogue in the reality of those who are at the bottom. Hence, Pope Francis talks about "places of encounter of mutual enrichment"[18] with "a holiness born of encounter and engagement, contemplation and services, receptive solicitude and life in community, cheerful sobriety and the struggle for justice."[19]

Although Pope Francis does not address global health issues related to the end of life, he offers resources for us to engage with those suffering in the local realities because of poverty, vulnerability to illnesses, lack of health care, and premature death. Francis's teaching leads us to engage with people like José and the Yanomami mothers to listen to their stories, contemplate their faces, and learn what is threatening their lives. This engagement creates a liberating path for justice in health care.

In his latest encyclical, *Fratelli tutti*, Pope Francis continues the development of this theology of encounter and listening to the poor. He addresses the COVID-19 pandemic and, thus, global health, with his challenge to the culture of indifference and individualism that kills any opportunity to rebuild the human family.[20] To rebuild this family in a globalized solidarity, Francis stresses the need of listening to others. "The ability to sit down and listen to others, typical of interpersonal encounters, is paradigmatic of the welcoming attitude shown by those who transcend narcissism and accept others, caring for them and welcoming them into their lives."[21] Then he adds:

> "When one part of society exploits all that the world has to offer, acting as if the poor did not exist, there will eventually be consequences. [...] Encounter cannot take place only between the holders of economic, political, or academic power. Genuine social encounter calls for a dialogue that engages the culture shared by the majority of the population."[22]

The poor are those who best embody and represent this population. They are those who suffer most because of the poverty, oppression, and exploitation that make them disproportionally more vulnerable to illnesses, deny them access to health care leading to premature death. This context and approach are very relevant for the end of life in global health because they show the most challenging issues for people's life and death, with a perspective that includes the voices of the poor and the oppressed.

3. Conclusion

In 1989, Brazilian theologian Márcio Fabri dos Anjos wrote a short essay for the newsletter Boletim ICAPS intitled "Eutanásia em Chave de Libertação" ('Euthanasia in a Liberating Key'). He argued that biomedical ethics had narrowed discussions about euthanasia in such a way that it did not capture end-of-life issues in countries marked by poverty, injustice, and oppression. Dos Anjos examined that the word "euthanasia" refers to a "good, happy death" for terminal patients. But it was also necessary to think about those "bad, unhappy deaths" because of lack of proper medical assistance and those deaths outside hospital contexts. Those deaths make us "think about slow and quiet deaths created by systems and structures."[23] Hence, he coined the neologism "misthanasia" to incorporate these slow and quiet deaths in our discussion on the end of life and bioethics. Dos

Alexandre A. Martins

Anjos said: "*Misthanasia* makes us think about those who died by hunger [...] make us think about the death of an impoverished person, embittered by the abandonment, because of the lack of the most basic resources."[24]

Misthanasia has become part of the bioethical vocabulary in Brazil to represent those deaths because of injustice, oppression and marginalization from accessing health care, and has a broader significance here.[25] It is a term that conveys the reality that most urgent end-of-life issues in global health are not related to individuals' autonomy to choose or refuse care while dying, but rather lie in the daily risks of falling ill and dying without the ability to reach any proper health care. Misthanasia, and not euthanasia, is truly occurring every day among the poor, particularly in the LMIC. Being at the bottom with those who experience this reality of the end of life seems an appropriate approach for global health in order to address the most urgent challenges toward life and death with dignity.

Notes

1. Norman Daniels/Bruce Kennedy/Ichiro Kawachi, "Health and Inequality, or, Why Justice Is Good for Our Health," in Sudhir Anand/Fabienne Peter/Amartya Sen (eds.), *Public Health, Ethics, and Equity*, New York: Oxford University Press, 2004, 63–92, here 65–66.
2. There are many comprehensive reports with studies showing the connection between poverty and illness. These reports are promoted by organizations, such as WHO, World Bank and The Lancet working teams, and can be found on their websites. See also: Nazim Habibov/Alena Auchynnikava/Rong Luo, "Poverty Does Make Us Sick," Annals of Global Health 85.1 (2019), 1–12, doi: 10.5334/aogh.2357.
3. Instituto Socioambiental, "Povos indígenas nos Brasil," at https://pib.socioambiental.org/pt/P%C3%A1gina_principal [29 March 2021].
4. Carlos Fausto, "O sarampo do tempo de meu avô: memórias do etnocídio na pandemia," *Nexo Jornal*, 24 april 2020, at https://www.nexojornal.com.br/ensaio/debate/2020/O-sarampo-do-tempo-de-meu-av%C3%B4-mem%C3%B3rias-do-etnoc%C3%ADdio-na-pandemia [29 March 2021].
5. Ministério da saúde, Secretaria Especial de Saúde Indígena (SESAI), at https://saudeindigena.saude.gov.br/corona [29 March 2021].
6. Ricardo Ventura Santos/Ana Lucia Pontes/Carlos E.A. Coimbra Jr., "Um fato social total: COVID-19 e povos indígenas no Brasil," Cadernos de saúde pública 36.10 (2020), 1–5, here 2, doi: 10.1590/0102-311X00268220 (my translation).
7. Redação, "Veja 10 declarações racistas de Bolsonaro sobre os indígenas," Esquerda Diário, 27 August 2019, at http://www.esquerdadiario.com.br/Veja-10-declaracoes-racistas-de-Bolsonaro-sobre-os-indigenas [29 March 2021].
8. Élio Gasda, "Os mortos não são números: Gerenciamento político da morte em tempos de pandemia," Annales FAJE 5.4 (2020), 40–49, here 43.
9. Gasda, "Os mortos não são números," 45–46.

10. John Paul II, *Evangelium vitae*, 25 March 1995, at https://www.vatican.va/content/john-paul-ii/en/encyclicals/documents/hf_jp-ii_enc_25031995_evangelium-vitae.html [19 July 2021], no. 65.
11. Congregation for the Doctrine of the Faith, *Samaritanus Bonus: On the Care of Persons in the Critical and Terminal Phases of Life*, 14 July 2020, at https://www.vatican.va/roman_curia/congregations/cfaith/documents/rc_con_cfaith_doc_20200714_samaritanus-bonus_en.html [29 March 2021].
12. John Paul II, *Evangelium vitae*, no. 3.
13. Francis, *Evangelii gaudium*, 24 November 2013, at https://www.vatican.va/content/francesco/en/apost_exhortations/documents/papa-francesco_esortazione-ap_20131124_evangelii-gaudium.html [19 July 2021], no. 49.
14. Francis, *Evangelii gaudium*, no. 193.
15. Francis, *Evangelii gaudium*, no. 198.
16. Francis, *Evangelii gaudium*, no. 199.
17. Francis, *Laudato si'*, 24 May 2015, at https://www.vatican.va/content/francesco/en/encyclicals/documents/papa-francesco_20150524_enciclica-laudato-si.html [19 July 2021], no. 196.
18. Francis, *Querida amazonia*, 2 February 2020, at https://press.vatican.va/content/salastampa/en/bollettino/pubblico/2020/02/12/200212c.html [19 July 2021], no. 30.
19. Francis, *Querida amazonia*, no. 77.
20. Francis, *Fratelli tutti*, 3 October 2020, at https://www.vatican.va/content/francesco/en/encyclicals/documents/papa-francesco_20201003_enciclica-fratelli-tutti.html [19 July 2021] no. 222.
21. Francis, *Fratelli tutti*, no. 48.
22. Francis, *Fratelli tutti*, no. 219.
23. Márcio Fabri dos Anjos, "Eutanásia em chave de libertação," *Boletim* ICAPS 7.57 (1989), 6–7, here 6 (my translation).
24. Dos Anjos, "Eutanásia em chave de libertação," 7 (my translation).
25. Luiz Antonio Lopes Ricci, *A morte social: mistanásia e bioética*, São Paulo: Paulus, 2017. Ricci argues that the concept of *misthanasia* allows us to include a prophetic demission to bioethics, leading this discipline to thinking and acting against structures that create social vulnerability and marginalization from access to health care (Ricci, *A morte social*, 20).

Assisted Suicide:
A Rational Option or a Tragedy?

JEAN-PIERRE WILS

In the context of the debate about assisted dying, assisted suicide is increasingly coming to the fore. In the Netherlands and Germany there will shortly be a revision of the penal code, and help with suicide is to be expressly allowed. Under this law the autonomy of the person concerned – their right to self-determination in matters relating to death – must be respected. There are no decisive arguments against a demand for assisted suicide, but the one-sided focus on autonomy involves considerable dangers. Suicide should not be glorified as an act of overdue emancipation. It is no enhancement of personal freedom, but a tragedy.

1. Looking at suicide

At the end of his book *You Must Change your Life,* Peter Sloterdijk wrote: 'A carefully managed and fostered death is a direct revolt against dying like an animal, which Job described as the fate of human beings.'[1] But the fight against the involuntary nature of death – shaping dying as one's own show -, he argues, is a civilising task. A human being's 'departure from their self-incurred immaturity', as Kant put it, still has to be achieved in matters of death. Here the Enlightenment has not succeeded in getting a real hearing, but the signs of change are unmistakable. 'A modern sign of this civilising movement is the growing suicide movement in the West.'[2]

Sloterdijk's view is representative of what is (for now) the last stage of a movement for emancipation in matters of dying. Dying, which indeed was for too long surrounded by medical and state paternalism, must now, he argues, to be brought into the realm of our own action. So-called 'active euthanasia', being killed on demand by a third person, was always related to the action of another person. In other to reduce this dependency, left 'to the end', he says that what must be in the truest sense of the word the last possible action, procuring one's own death, must now be brought into focus. The triumph of the Enlightenment is made complete when the idea of autonomy becomes a reality in the face of this last frontier.[3] Liberalisation of assistance around dying – for example, the acceptance of a suicide brought about by the assistance of doctors following clear medical criteria – is necessary. But in the meantime a strangely euphoric attitude is spreading with regard to a radical liberation of help with suicide. The last stretches of the peak of autonomy may now be scaled.

In her thoughtful essay 'Mein Tod gehört mir: Über selbstbestimmtes Sterben' ('My Death belongs to me: On Self-determined Death'), Svenja Flaßpöhler has asked the frightening question whether the unavoidable wish for autonomy that characterises the modern individual, does not have a dialectical reverse side, 'an independence that can no longer be distinguished from isolation'.[4] And she adds another question:

> 'But what does it mean against this background, when people in the last phase of their existence turn to another person – only for their support to depart from life? What does it mean that we are thinking about help to take our own life at a time in which the right of an individual to take their own decisions counts as one of the highest values of our culture? Is this a sign of the long overdue breaching of the taboo of the death wish that leads to a thoroughly humane sociality of death? Or is assisted suicide rather the manifestation of the modern, occasionally forcefully emerging, desire to determine even what is unavailable, the moment and the form of one's own death? Is assisted suicide the last (despairing) assertion of our own agency?'[5]

In the last few years suicide has been a central topic of public attention. For centuries suicide was regarded as something done in extremis. The decision to do violence to oneself was surrounded generally by an atmosphere of gloom. A person who took the decision to 'put an end to their life' had by that action to some extent decided to excommunicate themselves from the community of the living. They were marked with the stain of having crossed the final boundary – the apparently iron law of nature, self-preservation, *conservatio sui*. The comparatively tolerant attitude of the ancient world gave way to a strict Christion prohibition, which only began to waver with the beginning of the modern period. In a slow process suicide was freed from this moral judgment and the criminalisation that resulted from this. It was only after it had been subjected to a process of medicalisation and subsequent psychologization, however, that there began a process of which we are at the provisional end. What has happened is that suicide has been ennobled as a rational option. There has been a normalisation. It took a long time for the taboo on suicide to be breached; in fact, it has only taken place in the very recent past.

'The question of suicide,' says the cultural studies scholar Thomas Macho, 'is a one of the key themes of the modern period. Since the fin de siècle, and certainly since the end of the Second World War, the radical revaluation of suicide – on the one hand the process of the lifting of the taboo, on the other the popularisation of an emancipatory "creation of the self" – has taken place in several areas of culture.[6]

In the context of the discussion, assisted dying suicide has evidently risen to the status of an 'ultimate emanicpation'.[7] It really looks as though we are living in an 'age of increasing fascination with suicide'.[8] In the last twenty years suicide has a acquired a place as a political manoeuvre in attacks and radical protests, as a theme in cinema, literature and philosophy, and not least a prominent place in public consciousness as a central topic in the assisted dying debate.

In Germany this happened very dramatically when the Federal Constitutional Court, in its decision on 26 February 2020, declared the 'hitherto' strict regulation of assisted suicide to be null and void. Article 217 of the penal code, which prohibited so-called professional assistance with suicide, that is, assistance that was designed to be repeated, was repealed. The court based its argument on a 'right to self-determined death'.

(a) The right to a self-determined death includes the freedom to take one's own life. Where an individual decides to end their own life, having reached this decision based on how they personally define

quality of life and a meaningful existence, their decision must, in principle, be respected by state and society as an act of personal autonomy and self-determination.
(b) The freedom to take one's own life also encompasses the freedom to seek and, if offered, make use of assistance provided by third parties for this purpose.[9]

In the detailed exposition of the judgment one sentence stands out particularly: 'The right to suicide, however, prohibits the subordination of the permissibility of suicide assistance to material criteria, for example to make it dependent on the presence of an incurable disease.'[10]

The judgment, whose effects on policy are still awaited as this article goes to press, more or less threw the previous restrictive policy on assisted dying in Germany out of the window. The so-called active or direct assistance with suicide, that is, the killing of a person at their request by a third party, was and continues to be forbidden. Assisted suicide was not legally forbidden in the strict sense, but the penal code had erected such high barriers that the possibility of such help in practice was excluded. The doctors' professional code assumed that such assistance was not a task for a doctor and should therefore not be undertaken.

Compared with other jurisdictions internationally, with this judgment the federal constitutional court has leaped into the front line of the liberalising movement in rebus mortis. This can easily be seen from the text just quoted. Autonomy in the sense of taking one's own decisions is the central ethical category that forms the basis of the whole argument. The object of the decision-making is 'quality of life' and 'the meaningfulness of one's own existence'. In this context the use of 'material criteria' to assess the permissibility of the suicide assistance is rejected. The monopoly exercised by autonomy is striking. This means that the decision is guided by a subjective standard: judgments about the quality of one's own life are intrinsically dependent on the individual concerned, statements about 'meaningfulness' even more so. Against this background it is logical to dismiss the use of 'material criteria', since the introduction of medical or psychological symptoms would presuppose a meta-subjective perspective. There is no need for a serious illness or a terminal state to be diagnosed.

With this view of things the judgment has allied itself with the 'suicide avant-garde', which in the Netherlands is fighting to have assisted suicide largely permitted:

With the slogan 'a completed life', a bill is before the Netherlands parliament, presented by the D66 party and drafted by the parliamentarian Pia Dijkstra, whose focus is almost entirely on this subjective perspective. The arguments of the German federal constitutional court in some passages are almost word for word identical.[11]

An ethical and legal language game has obviously been set up that has little desire to consider additional or alternative viewpoints. Anyone thinking about assisted dying clearly has to go through the eye of the needle of this narrow category construct. At the other end they will meet the 'end-of- life accompanier', who, having undergone special training, is able to practice his or her assistance. There is no need for these experts to be doctors; after all, when the medical basis for a decision has been removed, they are no longer professionally involved. Carers, psychotherapists or health psychologists take their place.

We have already used the term normalisation. What does it mean? In the framework of the discussion about assisted dying the tragic element of suicide – the self-extinction of a person out of despair – has increasingly faded into the background in favour of a reinterpretation of it as a rational choice about the ending of one's life. Suicide has become an option suggested by our reason. No longer is it burdensome illnesses that bring such a choice into view, but the negative judgment of the person concerned about the quality and meaning of continuing their life. Obviously such a judgment does not drop out of a clear blue sky. In the vast majority of cases it is the product of a piling up of grievances, complaints about dependence and limitations. These can of course to some degree be presented as objective. But they are not crucial. Such 'material criteria' are not decisive. What is decisive is the individual's judgment about whether he or she still wants to go on living. And this subjective assessment that to carry on living is not desirable must be respected. It is the duty of the state to dismantle any obstacles to this. This programme is correctly described as normalisation.

Assisted suicide has been discussed in detail, and in recent years not only by civil society and politicians, but also continually in academic circles.[12] This extremely necessary debate has been conducted mainly with ethical and legal arguments. At the centre of such discussions is the question what actions should be allowed or prohibited for what ethical considerations or those of criminal law. This is the right focus because in matters of assisted dying the existing rules, but especially the intended changes, demand convincing justifications. This legal and ethical analysis, however, needs to be broadened to include a diagnosis from the philosophy of culture that investigates the very different question of why we are obviously living in an 'age of growing fascination with suicide'.[13]

2. Real fictions of Optimisation

The debate about assisted suicide is to a very large extent marked by the logic and dynamic of the media in which it occurs. If you do not excite attention you are overlooked in digital media.[14] Without being willing to adapt to the speed at which information is disseminated, one is marginalised. The 'pressure for cognitive change' exerted by the internet on its users is powerful.[15] The pull of the internet and its addictive potential are obvious.[16] They format the personalities of internet and media users. Their sphere of experience undergoes what the literary critic Albrecht Koschorke called 'remodelling'.[17] The images that circulate today in dizzying diversity and with penetrating obtrusiveness demand to be replicated in the lives of consumers. There is widespread communication about suicide in social media that propagates ideas of autonomy with regard to death.

Our lives must be led in the best possible way and as far as possible under our own control. We ought to follow a path led by autonomous and independent decisions, a path that will also end under the banner of self-determination – at the moment of death. The atmosphere of self-optimisation has meanwhile fallen like blight over all segments of life. This self-perfection can never start too soon, but it can definitely end too soon. When it first appeared, the ideal of self-optimisation may have been an abstract demand, like a strange fiction that showed life in a new light, one which seemed to indicate a high degree of artificiality. But a person who is constantly confronted with such an ideal, at some point begins to internalise it. Real behaviour starts to follow the model, and there is an 'interplay of conditioning and self-conditioning' that creates what Ulrich Bröckling has called a 'real fiction'.[18]

The idea of self-optimisation calls for a life in activist mode. Anyone who wants to follow this model must ban all accidents and unpredictability from their existence. A sort of 'rage against contingency' has spread, which seeks to subordinate all phases of life to a plan and precautionary regulation. 'You can never take enough precautions and never too early,'[19] which is why the fact of death must as far as possible be transformed into a piece of information in the biography, its last piece. In this context preparation for death means provision for death on one's own terms, putting into practice the ideal of self-realisation even during the very last phase of life.[20] This model produces a normative expectation. Anyone who would like to lead a self-determined life, must do so in accordance with this norm. Anyone who does not want to die on someone else's terms must prepare for an authentic death, that is, a death in accordance with the norm of autonomy. In this context preparing for death means allowing for a self-determined death, putting into practice the ideal of self-realisation even in the last stage of life.[21] In an important study, Nina Streek has has highlighted this paradoxical effect of the ideal of autonomy and authenticity: we feel obliged to exercise autonomy, and authenticity is a demand:

> The effort to improve the process of dying developed... a self-destructive dynamic, as the concern to allow everyone to have their 'own death', a death matching individual ideas, was distorted and became an institutionalised model of the expectation of remaining oneself even in death. 'Be authentic!' That is the imperative the dying person finds themselves confronted with today. In the wake of the development of palliative care and the assisted dying organisations, the guiding principle of authenticity, which these movements constantly promoted, lost its original meaning and no longer encouraged the creation of new freedoms to choose how one might die, but on the contrary served to narrow individual freedoms.[22]

3. Autonomy and Liberalism

The language of autonomy as the ideal is the privileged language of present-day ethics. The French sociologists Luc Bolstanski and Laurent Thévenot are surely right in talking about a dominant 'model of a justifying order'.[23] Reasons for morally relevant decisions are taken from the from the autonomy supply. In this context the idea of autonomy fund in John Stuart

Mill has supplanted the clearly more restrictive variant from the Kantian tradition. It is not the *limitations* on our actions imposed by practical reason that are decisive, but the *permissions* claimed by the liberally minded subject for its behaviour. These naturally include the freedom to design one's own death. Personal and private emancipation is here the dominant value. Autonomy has become an imperative of individuality, the challenge to free oneself from traditional social ties and lead one's life as far as possible in accordance with one's own ideas and decisions.

What is there to object to in this 'freeing of individuals from the cage of roles imposed by the institutions', to their leaving behind the 'prison of dependence'?[24] Probably hardly anything. But the norm of liberation from duties imposed by roles and oppressive situations has in the course of time, and certainly since the 1970s, been gradually *depoliticised* and radically *individualised*. What captures the attention is less the political question of what it means to be free and how this freedom can, if need be, fought for and guaranteed, but the assertion that we *are* free. As free beings we have the right to be largely undisturbed by others and not harassed by social norms from advancing on the path of our self-realisation and personal development. This idea has always been the core of liberalism and has been – at a later time - to a considerable degree compatible with neoliberalism. 'Liberalism,' writes Christoph Menke, 'is a naturalism (or positivism) of freedom. It is only interested in removing the obstacles, or creating the conditions, for the freedom we in principle have, or already have as a 'seed', to develop.'[25]

Talk of autonomy in this context is becoming increasingly *self-referential*.[26] A sort of 'private autonomy' has come into being that has little concern about the environment in which it develops and what else it may be required to take into account. The priority is the ability to take decisions freely and the possibility of putting such decisions into practice. We are living along the tightrope of free acts of self- determination and the tightrope stretches into the very last phase. This is not at all unusual, certainly not in a society whose pathos of freedom stretches from macro-economic parameters all the way to the psychic make-up of the individual. An 'education for dying' has come into being that pushes us to depart this life freely and authentically. Assisted suicide now belongs to the legitimate, in principle unproblematic and rational, options for measuring up to the norms of dying.

4. The psycho-economy of the arguments and the assisted dying narrative

We have frequently referred to the more or less subtle pressures produced by the self-determination model. Autonomy becomes real when the person chooses from the generous supply of options the one they fancy. An autonomy that did not consist in the freedom to translate preferences into independent decisions and also to have the possibility to implement such a decision would not be autonomy. There must be options, possibilities to choose. And of course we also have to consider the price we charge for them. It is not at all obvious that the multiplication of options in fact expands the freedom of the individual. An environment of expanded possibilities for choosing also creates pressure to choose. A person who doesn't choose ends up as an exception. Or, more accurately, refusing to choose is treated as a sort of choice. With regard to our subject-matter – assisted dying measures in general and the regulation of assisted suicide in particular – this having to choose has serious consequences. In such a (cultural) environment, in which choosing is an everyday matter, the end of life is also pulled into the spectrum of options. I must take an attitude to my end. I must express an opinion on how I want to die.

Dying or wanting to go on living has now become the result of a decision I have taken. Just going on living, that is, going on living without having to offer a justification, is now becoming difficult. The US ethicist J. David Velleman even talks about damage that is done when people are required to make a choice about continuing to live. Velleman is here considering active assisted dying, but it would be easy to include assisted suicide in this quotation.

The most important way in which the option of euthanasia may harm patients, I think, is that it ill deny them the possibility of staying alive by default.... Once a person is given the choice between life and death, he will rightly be perceived as the agent of his own survival. hereas his existence is ordinarily viewed as a given for him — as a fixed condition with which he must cope — formally offering him the option of euthanasia will cause his existence thereafter to be viewed as his doing.[27]

Assisted Suicide: A Rational Option or a Tragedy?

In the light of the forthcoming revised regulations on assisted suicide in Germany, in the Netherlands and many other countries, caution is therefore advisable. A normalisation of (assisted) suicide along the lines of the development described here is anything other than desirable. There is a need for clear criteria, with exceptions in individual cases treated with leniency. But suicide is in no sense a rational option. It represents a loss of a good, the loss of life. People who want to give up their lives are thus in the middle of what is perhaps the greatest tragedy that can befall anyone. Nothing is good any more. Going on living is a hassle. There are good reasons for trying to ensure that the number of such fates is as small as possible. Anything else would be a defeat – for all of us.

Translated by Francis McDonagh

Notes

1. Peter Sloterdijk, *Du musst dein Leben ändern: Über Anthropotechnik*, Frankfurt am Main, 2009, pp 665–666. English edition: *You Must Change Your Life*, Cambridge, 2013.
2. Peter Sloterdijk, *Du musst dein Leben ändern*, pp 665–666.
3. Jean-Pierre Wils, *Das Nachleben der Toten: Philosophie auf der Grenze*, Paderborn, 2019.
4. Svenja Flaßpöhler, *Mein Tod gehört mir. Über selbstbestimmtes Sterben*, Munich, 2013, p.18.
5. Flaßpöhler, *Mein Tod gehört mir*, p. 18.
6. Thomas Macho, *Das Leben nehmen: Suizid in der Moderne*, Berlin, 2017, p. 8.
7. See Jean-Pierre Wils, *Sich den Tod geben: Suizid als letzte Emanzipation?*, Stuttgart, 2021.
8. Macho, *Das Leben nehmen*, p. 15.
9. See https://www.bundesverfassungsgericht.de/SharedDocs/Entscheidungen/EN/2020/02/rs20200226_2bvr234715en.html (the court's own English version, accessed 15/10/2021).
10. See https://www.bundesverfassungsgericht.de/SharedDocs/Pressemitteilungen/EN/2020/bvg20-012.html (Accessed 15/10/2021. I have retranslated the court's English version in the light of the original German, Translator).
11. Bill proposed by the member Pia Dijkstra concerning the end of life accompaniment by others on request with regard to the Penal Code, the Law on professions involved in individual health care and other laws (Law regarding end of life accompaniment by others on request)) No 2 Bill, No 3 Explanatory memorandum, 35534, at: https://www.eerstekamer.nl/behandeling/20200717/memorie_van_toelichting/document3/f=/vlafha7mfuyh.pdf [Accessed 16/10/ 2021].

12. See especially Héctor Wittwer, *Das Leben beenden: Über die Ethik der Selbsttötung*, Paderborn, 2020.
13. Macho, Das Leben nehmen, p. 15.
14. See Andreas Bernard, *Komplizen des Erkennungsdienstes: Das Selbst in der digitalen Kultur*, Frankfurt, 2017.
15. Frank Schirrmacher, *Payback: Warum wir im Informationszeitalter gezwungen sind, zu tun, was wir nicht wollen, und wie wir die Kontrolle über unser Denken zurückgewinnen*, Munich, 2009, p. 60.
16. Reports about the speed at which dependence on digital technology is growing are alarming. See Adam Alter, *Unwiderstehlich: Der Aufstieg suchterzeugender Technologien und das Geschäft mit unserer Abhängigkeit*, Munich, 2018.
17. Albrecht Koschorke, *Körperströme und Schriftverkehr: Mediologie des 18. Jahrhunderts*, Munich, 2003, p. 162.
18. Ulrich Bröckling, *Das unternehmerische Selbst: Soziologie einer Subjektivierungsform*, Frankfurt, 2007, p. 35.
19. Günther Anders, ,'Die Weltfremdheit des Menschen', in: *Günther Anders, Die Weltfremdheit des Menschen: Schriften zur philosophischen Anthropologie*, Munich, 2018, pp 11–47, quotation from p. 28.
20. Ulrich Bröckling, 'Prävention: Die Macht der Vorbeugung', in: *Ulrich Bröckling, Gute Hirten führen sanft: Über Menschenregierungskünste*, Berlin, 2017, pp 73–112, quotation from p. 79.
21. Vgl. Magnus Schlette, *Die Idee der Selbstverwirklichung: Zur Grammatik des modernen Individualismus*, Frankfurt, 2013.
22. Nina Streeck, *Jedem seinen eigenen Tod: Authentizität als ethisches Ideal am Lebensende*, Frankfurt, 2020, p. 283.
23. Luc Boltanski and Laurent Thévenot, *Über die Rechtfertigung: Eine Soziologie der kritischen Urteilskraft*, Hamburg, 2014, p. 96. English edition: *On Justification. Economies of Worth*, Princeton and Oxford, 2006.
24. Ulrich Beck, 'Begriff und Theorie reflexiver Modernisierung', in: *Ulrich Beck, Die Erfindung des Politischen: Zu einer Theorie reflexiver Modernisierung*, Frankfurt, 1993, pp 57–98, quotations from p. 63; English edition: *The Reinvention of Politics: Rethinking Modernity in the Global Social Order*, Cambridge 1997.
25. Christoph Menke, 'Die Lehre des Exodus. Der Auszug aus der Knechtschaft', in: *Christoph Menke, Am Tag der Krise: Kolumnen*, Cologne, 2018, pp 77–93, quotation from p. 80.
26. See Heiner Bielefeldt, 'Entleerung der Autonomie: Zum Urteil des Bundesverfassungsgerichts über Suizidassistenz', *Stimmen der Zeit* 8 (2020), 563–572.
27. J. David Velleman, 'Against the Right to Die', in *J. David Velleman, Beyond Price: Essays on Birth and Death*, Cambridge, 2015, pp 5–21, quotation from p.12.

The Filipino Family and Health Care Decision-making at the End of Life

ERIC MARCELO O. GENILO

In the Philippines, the family acts as a caregiver, patient advocate, and primary decision-maker on matters related to the care of those dying or seriously ill. Patients take on a passive role and readily accept a loss of autonomy as they entrust themselves entirely to their family's care. Religious beliefs and cultural values present obstacles to discussions about advanced directives. Filial piety, a religious duty to preserve the gift of life, and a belief in God as the arbiter of life and death are factors that influence Filipino families to leave in God's hands the time and manner of a person's death. Aggressive medical interventions are often favored over withholding or removing extraordinary means to sustain life for terminal patients. Filipino families are expected to do everything to extend the terminally ill patient's life until God chooses to intervene and end the patient's suffering. Covid-19 protocols present severe challenges to the practice of family-centered health care by limiting the amount of contact and care the family can provide for members infected with the virus.

The Farewell, a 2019 American-Chinese movie by Lulu Wang filmed in modern-day China, tells the story of a family whose beloved grandmother, Nai Nai, has been diagnosed with terminal cancer. The family prevented Nai Nai from knowing about her condition. To give her extended family members a reason to come home and see their dying grandmother, the family organized an elaborate wedding banquet. A granddaughter, Billi, who lives in New York, goes back to China to see Nai Nai and struggles with the secrecy imposed by her family. Her family explained that unlike in the United States, where people deal with death as individuals, Chinese families deal with dying communally. The dying person is spared the knowledge of the diagnosis while the rest of the family takes up the emotional burden of dealing with the illness and impending death. The secrecy was less an act of deception and more of an expression of filial love and sacrifice.[1] Lulu Wang, the movie's director, based the story on her family's response to her real grandmother's diagnosis of terminal lung cancer. She says that such a decision to withhold medical information from a family member is not uncommon in China.

While the Philippines, a predominantly Catholic country, does not share the Confucian belief system of many of the movie's characters, Filipino families also respond to grave or terminal illness similarly. Bioethicist Josephine Lumitao notes the religious beliefs, cultural values, and social realities that shape how Filipino families care for their ill and infirmed members: "The central role of the family, high costs of health care, the cultural traits of fatalism, utang na loob (debt of gratitude), caring, and the deep religiosity of the Filipino patient result in an interplay of factors that may conflict with Western ethical principles of autonomy and informed consent."[2]

1. Family-centered Decision-making

In times of illness, the Filipino family acts as a patient advocate. Personal medical information about a patient is shared among family members who dutifully provide financial assistance, emotional accompaniment, and physical care. The family protects the sick member from stress and anxiety by filtering or withholding medical information. Even if a patient asks about their condition, the family still decides whether the patient is ready to be given accurate and complete information or if a more benign version is needed.[3] For example, euphemisms are used, such as *bukol* (mass) to refer to cancer and "weak lungs" to describe pulmonary tuberculosis, to temper the gravity of the diagnosis and spare the patient from anxiety.[4]

Filipino physicians communicate directly to family members rather than the patient and often accede to the family's request to withhold medical information from the patient. Within this family-centered system of health care decision-making, the principles of autonomy, confidentiality, and informed consent are set aside. These bioethical principles emphasize an individual's independence and agency on health matters. Filipino culture emphasizes a person's connection to and dependence on a network of family and community relationships that form a protective environment in difficult times. Filipino patients take on a passive role and readily accept their loss of autonomy as they entrust themselves entirely to their family's care.[5]

Generally, the family's dominant authority figures decide on the patient's treatment. However, extensive consultation and negotiation among family members occurs before a decision is made. This decision-making process can last for an extended period, especially when there is disagreement over various treatment options. The family tries to achieve consensus on medical interventions because of the importance Filipinos place on smooth interpersonal relationships. The family wants to avoid conflict or resentment from members whose opinions were not considered. Disagreements among family members can delay medical interventions and prolong the patient's suffering.

A complicating factor that affects this family-centered decision-making is migration. More than ten percent of Filipinos are working or living abroad. Family members living outside the country are still considered part of the decision-making process for the patient's care. When someone in the family is dying, a family member living abroad will often request that all efforts be made to keep the patient alive until they can come home. The migrant will send money, if necessary, to pay for life-sustaining measures. Decisions to withdraw extraordinary means to sustain life are postponed until the absent family member arrives. This practice places a heavy burden on the patient and the family by prolonging the patient's stay in the hospital (often in the intensive care unit), which leads to the increased cost of medical care and added burdens for family members.[6] The patient may request to forego or cease treatment and hospitalization to avoid prolonged suffering and conserve the family's resources. Such patient requests are often rejected by family members who promise to do whatever they can to extend their lives. The cultural trait of *utang ng loob* (loosely translated as "debt of gratitude") influences the family to prefer aggressive treatment for terminally ill parents or elders. Filipino children "grow up with a deeply ingrained sense that they owe their lives and their whole being primarily to God and only secondarily to their parents."[7]

Adult children express their gratitude to their parents by providing them the best possible care when they become old, sick, and infirm. A decision to forego or withdraw extraordinary measures to prolong a terminally ill parent's life may be viewed as a failure of the children to honor and reciprocate their parent's love.

The high cost of hospitalization, medicine, and treatment in the country is often out of reach for many Filipinos. While the Philippines' poverty rate has been annually declining, the World Bank still projected an 18.7% poverty rate in 2021.[8] Concerns about the cost of modern medical treatment lead some families to favor non-traditional or indigenous medical practices first before turning to western medicine as a last resort. The family can influence a patient's compliance with medical advice.[9] For example, family members sometimes insist that a patient use a herbal treatment from a traditional healer to substitute for or to use alongside a prescribed medicine from a health professional. Such interventions by the family can lead to unintended medical complications.

2. Advanced Directives and Filipino Religiosity

Advanced directives can facilitate the decision-making process of families regarding end-of-life situations. However, discussion about death is taboo in many Asian cultures. Filipino families are protective of their sick or elderly members. They will choose to avoid any talk of death because the topic may be upsetting and because of the cultural belief that speaking of death will make it come true.[10] Even when a seriously ill patient wants to give instructions for their end-of-life care, they are discouraged by family members because it is viewed as a sign of resignation and a premonition of death.

Filipino religiosity also plays a role in the avoidance of any advanced preparation for death:

> "Filipino patients may not want to discuss end-of-life care because these exchanges demonstrate a lack of respect for the belief that individual fate is determined by God. If their hopes are shattered, patients are no longer able to enjoy their daily lives and may feel they are '... among the dead while still alive.'"[11]

Filipino Catholics consider life as a gift from God with a predetermined duration for each person. When a person dies of an illness, accident, or old age, family members will console one another, saying *panahon na niya* (it is his/her time) or *kinuha na siya ng Diyos* (God took him/her). The Filipino expression *bahala na ang Diyos* (God will take care of it) reflects an acceptance of God's dominion over one's life. It expresses a fatalism that entrusts to God all of life's difficulties and challenges.[12] This *bahala na* attitude can discourage discussions about withdrawing extraordinary means to sustain life. A perceived religious duty to preserve the gift of life and a belief in God as the arbiter of life and death influences Filipino families to leave in God's hands the time and manner of a person's death. Filipino families are expected to do everything to sustain the terminally ill patient's life until God chooses to intervene and end the patient's suffering. Filipinos believe that "divine intercession is the most effective advance directive they can hope for."[13] Ending aggressive treatment may be seen as a human intervention that violates God's prerogative to decide when a patient's life should end.

Filipinos have a common misunderstanding about the difference between euthanasia and withdrawing extraordinary means to sustain life:

> "In certain cultures, such as the Philippines, measures such as removing the ventilator and giving opioids could be perceived as tantamount to killing the patient; indeed, it may be equated with mercy-killing. As euthanasia is unacceptable in a country where the majority is Christian, this misperception can be a barrier to decisions to limit life-sustaining therapy in a dying patient; the result may include preventable negative consequences such as family caregiver strain and financial difficulties brought about by high hospital bills."[14]

It is only when the family's financial resources are depleted or the patient's suffering is no longer bearable that the cessation of aggressive treatment is considered as an option. In some cases, the family delays too long, and the patient eventually dies before a decision is made. Such a death is then interpreted as a form of divine intervention that ends a patient's suffering and relieves the family of the emotionally difficult decision to end extraordinary or disproportionate treatment.

3. Faith-based Responses to Illness

A deeply-rooted belief in the power of prayer, divine intervention, and miraculous healing provides devout Filipino Catholic patients and their families with the spiritual resources to face grave illness with hope for a favorable outcome.

In a study of Filipina-American survivors of breast cancer, Regina Lagman and colleagues highlighted the importance of prayer for the study participants. "Through prayer, they gained a comforting peace of mind by trusting God to care for their illness and to provide illness with deeper meaning. They believed healing power could be received from God and from other people's prayers."[15] Families commit themselves to pray for their sick members and enlist friends, acquaintances, and prayer groups to intercede to God for healing. Confidentiality about a patient's medical condition is set aside in favor of creating a network of "prayer warriors," with the hope that more prayers will ensure a favorable response from God.

In pre-Covid-19 times, healing masses and prayer services in parishes are well-attended. Patients and their families undertake pilgrimages to local Catholic shrines or the shrines of Fatima and Lourdes if they have the financial means. Priests are requested to visit patients in hospitals and homes to administer the sacrament of anointing of the sick or celebrate private masses for the patient and their families. Family members even pressure some patients to confess to a priest, believing that illness may be a form of divine punishment and that forgiveness of sins can bring about healing.

Belief in the power of prayer and the possibility of miraculous healing provide a source of hope and consolation for patients and their families. However, such views can also reinforce the *bahala na* attitude that places importance on divine intervention over medical treatment. Treatment might be delayed until certain religious activities such as pilgrimages or healing sessions have proven ineffective in producing a cure.

4. The Impact of Covid-19

The Covid-19 pandemic and the safety protocols implemented to address it significantly impact Filipino families' response to illness. Nursing homes are not typical in the country. Families prefer to take care of their elderly members at home. There is a higher risk of Covid-19 infection for the aged who share the same living space with extended family members. As social distancing protocols were implemented, the elderly are sometimes separated from their families and other sources of psychological and spiritual support such as community gatherings and religious celebrations. Adherence to Covid-19 prevention practices such as mask-wearing, hand-washing, and social distancing will depend on how seriously and consistently the family teaches its members to follow government-mandated health protocols.

When a family member tests positive for the virus, they are immediately informed of the diagnosis. The family has no opportunity to filter or hide the patient's diagnosis. Families are also unable to participate in the decision-making process for the patient's care. The local government decides where the person is to be quarantined and what form of care will be provided. The family's protective support structure is less accessible to the patient while he or she is confined in a hospital or a quarantine facility. Family members are no longer able to keep vigil with the Covid-19 patient to avoid infection. Covid-19 patients often have to deal with their illness alone without the usual physical accompaniment of their families. While some families can arrange online masses for patients in quarantine, the physical reception of the sacraments such as the Eucharist, confession, and anointing is not possible, adding to the patient's sense of separation from their faith community. The onset of symptoms in some patients and subsequent death happen so quickly that some families often cannot be present at the dying patient's last moments. Physically separated by quarantine protocols, bereaved family members cannot physically gather to support one another.

The effect of Covid-19 on economic activity has diminished Filipinos' capacity to provide adequate health care for their families. Not all persons can work from home and those who have to work outside run the risk of bringing the virus to their families, especially to their more senior and vulnerable members. An aggravating factor to the Covid-19 situation is natural disasters such as typhoons and floods that drive families to evacuation centers where social distancing is challenging to maintain, and the possibility of infection is higher.

Unlike more affluent countries in North America and Europe, the

Philippines struggles to procure enough vaccines for a population of 110 million people. The government assures that the vaccines they will buy and distribute will be safe and effective. However, a recent mishandling of a dengue vaccination program has fostered suspicion toward vaccines in general.[16] Once the Covid-19 vaccines are available, families will have to decide whether to have their elderly and vulnerable members vaccinated immediately or wait longer until their concerns about vaccine safety are addressed. Even during the Covid-19 pandemic, the family remains the primary patient advocate and the most significant decision-maker for health care.

5. Conclusion

The Filipino family is the primary health care decision-maker and source of emotional, social, and financial support of ill or dying patients. While the family provides a comprehensive safety net that takes care of a patient's needs, it can also limit the patient's capacity to access medical information and make decisions. Filipino cultural values emphasize the family's duty to care for its sick members with all available resources and to prolong their lives as much as possible. Filipino religious beliefs emphasize God's role as provider and final arbiter on matters of life and death, reinforcing a fatalistic view towards illness and death. Discussions about end-of-life situations and preparation for death are avoided or postponed as much as possible to avoid upsetting the patient and family members and to allow space for possible divine intervention.

The government's Covid-19 protocols present severe challenges to the practice of family-centered health care by limiting the amount of contact and care the family can provide for members who are infected with the virus. While the current pandemic makes it difficult for families to provide the usual level of care and accompaniment for their ill members, the family remains the primary source of support and assistance for patients.

Notes

1. Robert Ito, "A Family's Real-life Lie and the Movie That Complicated It," *The New York Times*, 5 July 2019, at https://www.nytimes.com/2019/07/05/movies/farewell-wang-awkwafina.html [2 November 2020].
2. Josephine M. Lumitao, "Death and Dying," in Angeles Tan-Alora/Josephine M. Lumitao (eds.), *Beyond a Western Bioethics: Voices from the Developing World*, Washington: Georgetown University

Press, 2001, 94–101, here 94.
3. Larry G. Kuan/Josephine Lumitao, "The Family and Health Care Practices," in Angeles Tan-Alora/Josephine M. Lumitao (eds.), *Beyond a Western Bioethics: Voices from the Developing World*, Washington: Georgetown University Press, 2001, 23–29, here 24.
4. Kuan/Lumitao, "The Family and Health Care Practices," 25.
5. Kuan/Lumitao, "The Family and Health Care Practices," 24–25.
6. Maria Fidelis Manalo, "Cultural and Family Structure Factors Affecting End-of-life Decision-making and End-of-life Care in the Philippines", at http://simul-europe.com/2017/mascc/Files/(lizamanalomd@gmail.com)CULTURAL_AND_FAMILY_STRUCTURE_FACTORS_AFFECTING_END%20OF%20LIFE%20DECISION%20MAKING.pdf [10 November 20202].
7. Kuan/Lumitao, "The Family and Health Care Practices," 26.
8. World Bank, Philippines Economic Update, October 2019, at https://www.worldbank.org/en/country/philippines/publication/philippines-economic-update-october-2019-edition#:~:text=Poverty%20reduction%20is%20expected%20to,%2C%20and%2018.7%25%20in%202021 [22 January 2021].
9. Kuan/Lumitao, "The Family and Health Care Practices," 25.
10. H. Russel Searight/Jennifer Gafford, "Cultural Diversity at the End-of-life: Issues and Guidelines for Family Physicians," *American Family Physician* 71.3 (2005), 515–522, here 518.
11. Searight/Gafford, "Cultural Diversity at the End-of-life," 518.
12. Regina A. Lagman/Grace J. Yoo/Ellen G. Levine/Kira A. Donnell/Holly R. Linn, "Leaving it to God: Religion, Spirituality, and Filipina American Breast Cancer Survivors," *Journal of Religion and Health* 53.2 (2014), 449–460, here 450–451.
13. Marcia Celine M. Abando/Sherwin O. Abril/Bella P. Maganaye/ Gracielle Joy D. Caringal/Maria Jocelyn B. Natividad/Shaine Katherine L. Otano, "Advanced Directives for Terminally Ill Patients: A Grounded Theory," *Asia Pacific Journal of Education*, Arts & Sciences 5.4 (2018), 1–9, here 7.
14. Maria Fidelis Coronel Manalo, "End-of-life Decisions about Withholding or Withdrawing Therapy: Medical, Ethical, and Religio-Cultural Considerations," *Palliative Care and Social Practice* 7 (2013), 1–5, here 4, doi: 10.4137/PCRT.S10796.
15. Lagman et al., "Leaving it to God," 454.
16. Chris Lo, "The Dengue Vaccine Dilemma," *Pharmaceutical Technology*, 16 December 2019, at https://www.pharmaceutical-technology.com/features/dangvaxia-philippines/ [19 July 2021].

Muslim Beliefs about Death: From Classical Formulations to Modern Applications

ABDULAZIZ SACHEDINA

Islamic law has preserved detailed accounts of religious aspects of death and dying. Shari'a has retained a continuity in its guidance regarding the religious and ritual aspects of death. Contemporary Muslim jurists have emphasized rulings that determine the moment of death and the permission to harvest organs. Even when the scriptural sources have provided detailed instructions about the funeral rites and mourning practices, as a rule, ethical analysis of the situation is dominated by extraction of a ruling. This paper highlights the religious and cultural issues that dominate the ethics of the end of life in Muslim traditions.

1. Introduction

The advent of new medical technologies in the last fifty years has rendered the task of defining death the most pressing issue in the field of biomedical ethics. Among Muslim jurists this involves an attempt to understand the moment of imminent death in brain-dead patients. Any error of judgment in this regard could lead to morally and legally questionable choices to end an individual's life by either actively or passively causing their death. However, the proper definition of death requires an understanding of the religious estimation of human life and an endeavor to unravel the secret of the soul (*nafs*) or the spirit (*ruh*) which, according to Muslim beliefs, is infused in the body and departs at the time of death.[1]

From an Islamic perspective, the determination of the time of death is essentially a religious-legal problem, not simply a medical or scientific one. Religious aspects of death are dominated by the doctrine that it is God, the giver of life and death, who knows the time of death, and death occurs upon the separation of the soul from the body. Strictly speaking, this separation is not open to direct empirical observation, and this is the major source of ambiguity in the community in determining the exact moment of death. Today, the traditional view of death, which focused upon the cessation of circulatory and respiratory activities as the criteria of the spirit's departure, has been overshadowed by the ability of new medical technologies to intervene by maintaining a patient's heartbeat, blood pressure, respiration, and liver and kidney functions within the normal range of values. Contemporary medical science has developed highly sophisticated techniques for determining the presence or absence of vital bodily functions. This possibility of restoring respiration or heartbeat even in the case of massive brain damage, when there is little likelihood of an individual recovering consciousness, has given rise to the problem of validating the possibility of cerebral death. In this article, I will summarize problems with the definition of death and the retrieval of organs in a cadaver as contemporary issues demanding that Muslim scholars and physicians undertake a dialogue to fully understand modern biotechnology and its impact upon defining death and the relationship humans have with their body.

2. Life and Death in Islamic Jurisprudence

Evidently, in the light of the lack of clear definitions in the Qur'an, there has been much speculation about the exact identification of the indicators of death. The exercise involves understanding the very essence of human life in the interaction between an ephemeral physical substance and an eternal entity that departs it at the time of death. That elusive component which transforms the human body into a living being is the spirit *(ruh)* or soul *(nafs)* which enters the fetus and ensouls it in the beginning of the embryonic journey to personhood, thereby effecting a change in the moral and legal status of the developing fetus. At the end of life, this substance leaves the body to return to its original source in the world of the spirits *('alam al-arwah)*. Just as the subject of the beginning of life in Islam raises questions about the exact timing when the spirit infuses the body to determine fetal inviolability, so at the end of life there is the challenge of determining without doubt when death has occurred.

There are two theories concerning the relationship between the physical body and the spirit. According to one, the reality of humankind is its spiritual substance or divine element, and the body is simply an instrument that serves this spiritual substance. According to this, the spirit is not something that resides in matter; rather, it is created by God as the source of life and linked to the body. This relationship is one of the spirit managing and having discretion over the body. According to Abu Hamid al-Ghazali (d. 1111) and other Sunni theologians, the spirit (*al-ruh*) is the subtle divine essence (*al-latifa al-rabbaniyya*), knowing, thinking and percipient, abiding in a human being; the concept is applied sometimes to the heart (*al-qalb*), the soul (*al-nafs*), and the intellect (*al-'aql*). The bodily parts are the tools of the spirit which enables the organs to perform different tasks and the heart to know the true nature of things. The "heart," as al-Ghazali explains, is merely another expression for the "spirit" which is able to learn and independently feel the emotions without any link to the bodily parts. When the body dies, the spirit is separated, and the ability of the body to function comes to a halt. [2]

Another theory regards the spirit as an attribute of life infused by God at the time of fetal ensoulment. In this sense, the spirit becomes identical with the body, and the body identical with the spirit, and from their union human personhood emerges.[3] The spirit as an attribute enables humans to gain knowledge, to feel the pains of sorrow as well as the pleasures of happiness. Death signifies the falling into disuse of the body because of the end of the spirit's control over the body and the end of the body's status as its tool. In the words of al-Ghazali: "Just as the onset of an incapacitating disease may mean that the hand is no longer a tool of which use is made, so death is an incapacitating disease spread throughout all members."[4]

Regardless of the nature of this relationship, the spirit, which is the source of the humanness of an individual, is actually the source of the personhood that begins when the spirit is infused in the body. What serves as the criterion of human life is the linkage between the rational spirit and the body. Thus, death is viewed as the permanent severance of the linkage between the rational spirit and the body, whether that linkage has been severed as a result of the spirit being liberated from the body because of its perfection, or as a result of the incapacitation of the body which prevents the spirit from penetrating the body barring it from its use.5 Cellular life alone cannot then serve as evidence for human life.

From the religious point of view, despite the fact that it is not known when exactly the spirit departs from the body, a number of criteria have been cited in the scriptural sources that indicate the separation of the spirit from the body when death occurs. Among these signs are the deterioration and ultimate decomposition of the body, the whitening of the skin, the sweating of the forehead, discharge of fluids from the eyes, discharge of sperm, slackening of the muscles, the contortion of the eyes, and wrinkling of the lips.[6] In medicine, death has been classified into two types, namely, physical and cellular death. The symptoms cited for the occurrence of each type correspond to those mentioned in the Islamic traditions.

Life and death are ultimately existential matters. Their correlation suggests a contradiction in terms since life indicates continuation of the blessings of living, while death points to extinction. The existential aspect of death that serves a critical purpose in relieving an individual from a lengthy period of suffering through illness or other afflictions can be discerned from the following verse of the Holy Qur'an that glorifies God for having created both life and death:

"Blessed be God in whose hand is the Kingdom –
God is powerful over everything –
who created death and life, so that God may try you
which of you is fairest in works." (Q. 67:1–2)

In this passage the act of creation is introduced as an external phenomenon, for which God is exalted, and which includes the creation of death as God's blessed activity, even though some commentators are of the opinion that since death suggests the opposite of what life indicates, there is ostensibly a contradiction in their correlation in creation.[7] However, no matter whether one holds that the correlation between life and death is contradictory because death signifies the negation of existence, or that life and death are both existential matters, there is absolutely no way of conceiving them as unrelated. They remain linked because to imagine a third possibility is impossible.

3. The Social-psychological Dimension of Death

With the new medical discussion regarding brain death, Muslim centers of juridical studies have correctly argued that investigation needs to go beyond the religious and juridical aspects of death to understand and deliberate on the suffering of those who are closely related to the patient. Serious illness overwhelms everyone in the family and demands a collective response to handle the pain and suffering of the patient, on the one hand, and the loss and separation following the imminent demise of the patient, on the other. The social-psychological dimension of death includes the way in which the family undertakes to preserve the dignity of the dead and the honor of those left behind. This includes avoiding all decisions that would lead to the desecration of the human body and safeguard respect for human personhood.

In this situation, brain-dead persons are the most vulnerable. Any procedure using newly dead patients for medical research and other humanitarian and educational purposes evokes reprehension. More critically, any suggestion to retrieve their organs is repugnant because the patient can no longer protect his/her dignity. In all Islamic communities, even when the patient had left a specific advance directive to permit the removal of organs to help those in urgent need of a transplant, the relatives cannot allow it because of the invasive postmortem procedures.

In the Islamic juridical tradition, a large number of rulings deal with the social and psychological implications of death for those who are left behind: parents, spouse, children, and other relatives. Muslim funeral traditions enable the relatives to cope with the loss of the loved one, even if it be a child, whose departure has become a major source of disruption in the normal familial life. Accordingly, the tradition deals with death on two levels: (1) at the formal level of rituals that must be performed for the dead by the family and the community; (2) at the legal level of rulings that outline the rights and duties of the immediate family members toward the dead and the survivors. Consequently, at the ritual level the Shari'a lays down the rules about the number of days the mourning should be held; the religious personages (the Prophet, the Companions, the Family) who should be remembered in these ceremonies; those who should bring food to the family of the dead; visitations of the graves in the cemetery; recitation of the Qur'an at the grave etc. Ghazali has aptly captured the spirit and purpose of these funeral rituals as encouraging people to visit the family members and console them for their loss.[8]

4. Withholding or Withdrawing Treatment? Who Decides?

The meaning of human life is grounded in the fact that it is sacred because God is its origin and its destiny. Death does not occur except by God's leave, as the Qur'an reminds humanity. At the same time the fact of diseases or trauma that cause death are recognized. Health care providers have an obligation to do all that is possible to prevent premature death. The question then is: is the goal of health care professionals to maintain life at any cost, or merely to provide comfort so that death may come as quickly and comfortably as possible? The question has wider implications because it evokes different and often competing ethical values in deciding the course of action or specific interventions that the situation demands. On the one hand, there is the obligation to save and prolong life; on the other, there is a call to limit life-sustaining treatment as required by principles of distributive justice in resource allocations. Nevertheless, the real question is the authority that can make such decisions. Who should draw the line between personal values and beliefs and the more objective medical analysis of health care providers? Should the financial burden of life-sustaining treatment ever dictate its termination?

The role of religious guidance in these and other matters related to most critical care decisions is to speak authoritatively about death and about self-imposed limits at the professional level regarding such matters. Medical judgments about death are usually based on probability. It is only very close to the time of death that physicians can predict the end with certainty. Hence, the Qur'an puts forward a harsh reminder to human beings that there are times when they need to recognize their own limits as humans and entrust nature to take its own course (Q. 39:42). The refusal to recognize the inevitability and naturalness of death leads to more aggressive life-saving interventions. At the same time, to withhold specific interventions at the most critical time leads to deliberate avoidance of the responsibility in administering the right treatment to save the patient's life.

For the past three decades scholars have struggled to identify the proper circumstances under which life-sustaining medical treatment should be limited. The phenomenal advancements in the field of medical technology have not allowed for the development of adequate procedures and processes to regulate their introduction and use in critical care settings. Although there seems to be a consensus among legal experts belonging to different schools of Islamic law about brain death that results from an irreversible destruction of the brain, the question that remains to be answered is a theological one connected with the location of human soul.

As mentioned before, the classical legal definition connects death with the traditional signs, including complete cessation of the heartbeat. Yet biological data about the function of the heart and other major activities connect life with the functions of the human brain. This discrepancy between the religious and contemporary scientific definition of death has generated even greater challenges for family members and health care professionals when making decisions about life-saving medical intervention, for instance, in the treatment of cardiopulmonary arrest, which is regarded as the final common pathologic-physiologic event in the process of dying. Failure to act immediately by undertaking CPR that involves external chest compression and some form of artificial respiration means certain death.

In Islamic social ethics an individual's welfare is intimately linked with his/her family and community. Accordingly, it is not the principle of autonomy that is evoked to determine a course of action in matters related to end-of-life decisions. Whether a physician can prolong life by introducing aggressive invasive treatments without causing further harm is decided by all connected with the patient. Yet, there are instances when the matter is referred to the religious leaders who provide prescriptive rulings connected with terminally ill patients to which I will now turn.

5. The Right to Die?
In Muslim culture, good health is God's blessing, and thus, whenever asked: "How are you?" (literally: How is your health?), a Muslim responds: "All praise is due to God!" However, this positive appraisal of good health might seem to suggest that illness is an evil that must be eliminated. No doubt illness is regarded as an affliction that needs to be cured by every possible legitimate means. In fact, the search for cures is founded upon the unusual confidence generated by the divine promise that God has not created a disease without creating its cure.[9] Hence, the

purpose of medicine and the primary obligation of a Muslim physician is to search for cures and provide the necessary care to those afflicted with disease. Decisions about ending the life of a terminally ill patient at her/his request are beyond the physician's moral or legal obligations. The Qur'an states in no uncertain terms that "it is not given to any soul to die, save by the leave of God, at an appointed time" (Q. 3:145). Moreover, "God gives life, and He makes to die" (Q. 3:156). And, hence, "A person dies when it is written" (Q. 3:185, 29:57, 39:42).

Death, then, comes at the appointed time, by God's permission. In the meantime, humans are faced with the suffering caused by illness. How is suffering viewed in Islam? Is it part of the divine plan to cause suffering? With what end?

6. Stewardship of the Human Body and Suffering

The discussion about the quality of life points to the cultural and religious attitudes regarding human existence and the control over life-and-death decisions when an individual is undergoing severe suffering and advanced medical treatments do not promise recovery. Furthermore, it underscores the view that the human being has the stewardship, but not ownership, of his/her body. The individual is merely the caretaker, the real owner being God, the Creator. It is one's duty to take all the necessary steps to preserve one's body in a manner that would assist in seeking the good of both this world and the next. In light of such a stipulation about the human duty toward his/her earthly existence in Muslim theology, the problem of human suffering through illness assumes immediate relevance. The Qur'an points out that suffering is a form of a divine test or trial to confirm a believer's spiritual station (Q. 2:153–157). More pertinently, it functions as an instrument in revealing God's purpose for humanity and in reminding us that ultimately it is to God that human life belongs and to God it will return. Accordingly, from this scriptural perspective, suffering cannot be regarded as evil at all. In a well-known tradition, the Prophet is reported to have said: "No fatigue, nor disease, nor sorrow, nor sadness, nor hurt, nor distress befalls a Muslim, even if it were the prick he received from a thorn, but that God expiates some of his sins for that."[10]

However, afflictions should not lead a person to lose hope, because despair stems from a lack of trust in divine mercy. Other traditions also recognize a religious purpose of illness and underline its function, as for other forms of suffering, as God's trial of the people and the cleansing effect of illness. Hence, in a tradition the Prophet says that the patient earns merits under these trials and can attain the rank of a true believer: "When God intends to do good to somebody, He afflicts him with trials."[11] In addition to this spiritual-moral dimension, suffering serves an educational purpose: caused by human misconduct, suffering serves as a form of punishment to expiate for a sin.

Disbelief in God's power to heal and restore health is the major source of human desperation. It is also regarded as the source of human arrogation of the rights of God. Experiencing severe and untreatable suffering caused by illness serves as a reminder of one's being deprived of the divine blessing of good health through one's disbelief in God. As such, suffering is a means of self-purification from sinful behavior. It is in this state that when afflicted with illness Muslims are advised to beseech God to forgive their sins. Rather than contemplating ways to end one's life, either by refusal of life-support treatment or by requesting to die with active assistance, a Muslim is required to pray for an opportunity to have a fresh start with restored health.

7. End-of-life Decisions in the Muslim Tradition

The belief in God's immutable decree is also revealed in Muslim ethics where not only the right to die is not recognized, but the right to be assisted in dying, whether through "passive" or "active" means, is also ruled out. It is important to clarify here that since God decides about the end of life, the Shari'a refuses to recognize an individual's right in this matter. However, it recognizes the possibility of arriving at a collective decision by those involved in providing health care, including the attending physician and the family. The ethical principle affirmed in most unequivocal terms by the Prophet states: "No harm shall be inflicted or reciprocated in Islam" *(la darar wa la dirar fi'l-islam)*.[12] This is the principle that lays down the rule to avoid causing harm or harassment to the patient. It also allows for important distinctions and rules about life-sustaining treatments in terminally ill patients. This includes the distinction between killing (active euthanasia) and letting die (passive euthanasia) which often underlies distinctions between suicide and forgoing treatment or between homicide and natural death. The principle of "No harm" in some ways functions like the principle of non-maleficence. It raises a critical moral question about the intention of the health care providers in foregoing life-sustaining treatment, whether such a decision can be regarded as a form of killing, and if so, whether it is assisted suicide or homicide. There is no immunity in Islamic law for the physician who unilaterally and actively decides to assist a patient to die.

It is important to restate that the justificatory force of the rulings on "allowing to die" through pain-relief treatment or by withholding or withdrawing life-sustaining treatments when it is certain that the disease is causing untreatable suffering, is contingent upon the well-informed consultation with the physician and all parties involved in the patient's treatment and wellbeing. Since Islamic legal deliberations ground morality as part of the spiritual response to God in interhuman relationships, purely individual acts to terminate life, whether by the patient or the assisting physician, are regarded as acts of disobedience against God. In the final analysis, besides the exceptions noted in the two situations, there are no grounds in Islam for the justifiable killing of a terminally ill person, whether through voluntary active euthanasia or physician assisted suicide.

In conclusion, discussions of appropriate Islamic guidelines on a number of contemporary medical issues, including organ donation, continue in many places, both within and outside Muslim-majority societies. We have seen that a well-established religious stance on death does not provide totally clear criteria on such matters as ascertaining when a life has ended. Medical breakthroughs, in turn, have created a number of new dilemmas. The Islamic tradition continues to provide a basis for ongoing efforts to guide patients, families and medical practitioners in making the critical decisions involved at the end of life.

Notes

1. The Qur'an uses the term *nafs* in the meaning of "personhood" rather than "soul."
2. Abū Hāmid Muhammad al-Ghazāli, *The Remembrance of Death and the Afterlife*, Cambridge: The Islamic Text Society, 1989, 122–123; For different views of Sunni scholars, see al-Barr, *Mawt al-qalb aw mawt al-dimāgh*, Jedda: al-Dār al-Sa'udiya, 1406/1986, 37–45.
3. Muhammad b. Umar al-Husayn al-Razi, *al-Tafsir al-kabir*, Cairo: al-Matba'a al-Bahiya a-Misriya, 1938, vol. 21, 45.
4. Ghazali, *The Remembrance of Death*, 123.
5. Hisham b. al-Hakam asked the Imam al-Sadiq if the spirit is other than the blood. The Imam

replied: "Yes, the spirit, as I have explained to you, is the substance from the blood. When the blood becomes cold [upon death] the spirit leaves the body." See Ahmad b. Ali b. Abi Talib al-Tabarsi, *al-Ihtijaj*, Beirut 1966, vol. 2, 97.

6. al-Barr, *Mawt al-qalb aw mawt al-dimagh*, 71–82 covers the Sunni views on the criteria and critically evaluates the errors that have crept into the Islamic as well as medical pronouncements of death. For the Shiite views see: al-Tabarsi, *al-Ihtijaj*, vol 2, 97; Muhammad b. Ya'qub b. Ishaq al-Kulayni, *al-Usul min al-Kafi*, Tehran 1392/1972 vol. 3, 134–135, vol. 3, 161–163; Ibn Babwayh, *'Ilal al-sharyi'*, Najaf: Maktaba al-Haydariya, 1965, vol. 1, 309, section 261.

7. al-Razi, *Tafsir al-kabir*, vol. 30, 54, writes: "It is said that life is a description for a person inasmuch as he can learn and act; the matter of death is different. Some say that it is actually a negation of this ability [to learn and to act]. We are of the opinion that this is a description of existence contrary to life and we argue that God, the Exalted says: 'He is the one who created death,' because non-existence (al-'adam) is not creatable [on its own]. This is the conclusion."

8. Ghazali, *The Remembrance of Death*, 99, 108, 111.

9. Bukhari, Muhammad b. Isma'il Sahih al, *Kitab al-Marda*, Chicago: Kazi Publications, 1976, vol. 7, Hadith 582.

10. *Ibid.*, Hadith 545.

11. *Ibid.*, Hadith 548.

12. The principle is regarded as the most important source of all decisions affecting interpersonal relationship. See Abdulaziz Sachedina, *Islamic Biomedical Ethics: Principles and Application,* New York: Oxford University Press, 2009, 66–75.

Ars Vivendi: Spirituality for the End of Life in the 21st century

MARÍA MARCELA MAZZINI

In the next few pages I am going to talk about what was known as Ars moriendi *in the 14th and 15th centuries and the great tasks these texts pose. Then I will propose an update on these topics, which will enable people in the 21st century to think about a good death.*

For some years now, I have been studying the topic of spirituality at the end of life.[1] Thanks to this experience, I have been in contact with many people involved in palliative care in Argentina.[2] What they taught me during these years is invaluable: nurses, doctors, volunteers, but above all, the guests, who are the main protagonists of that space. They taught me a lot about what happens at the end of the biography, and I encountered many spiritual practices and experiences, most of them lived in ways that I had not imagined. I understood that the most important questions, the ones whose answers define us, are the ones that are the most postponed. They are crucial; they are not macabre but profound and liberating. Thinking about death helps us to live better, with more meaning and, therefore, with more happiness. That is why I have entitled this text *Ars Vivendi*. Thinking about death helps us to live better.[3]

1. *Ars moriendi*
Ars moriendi are treatises articulated as stories or engravings, which circulated especially after the Black Death that struck Europe in the early 14th century. These treatises were especially popular in the 14th and 15th centuries. They are a simple, basic, and relatively quick method to prepare

to die well. The idea of the good death is deeply Christian and has its roots in the good thief who dies with Jesus (Lk 23:39-43); therefore, the tradition of asking for a good death is not a modern or medieval novelty. What is modern if the "methodization of that final moment"[4] is a method that was accelerated by the Black Death.[5]

These texts[6], known under the name of *Tractatus* or *Speculum artis bene moriendi*[7], reached an enormous diffusion. They circulated in two versions: long and short[8]. They are a kind of guide designed to show the practices, prayers, and attitudes that both the sick person and their family members and the priest or lay person who spiritually accompanied the dying person should adopt. The short text – which was sometimes accompanied by engravings for illiterate people – speaks of the five temptations of the devil: that the dying person despair, that they be vain, that they be impatient, that they lose their faith, or that they long for the past. Then, it talks about the celestial forces that help with the transition, according to the versions, one or several angels appear, some saints, the blessed Virgin, even the Trinity, helping the *moriens* to resist and strengthening them in faith, hope, patience, humility, and detachment from goods and affections, in order to finally let go of oneself as a child in the hands of God.[9]

The inhabitants of Europe in the fifteenth century had the experience of the expiration of all things and the abruptness of the loss: death, in fact, for them came suddenly almost all the time. This meditation on the end illuminates the present vitality.

2. An update of the *Ars Moriendi*

As I write this text, the whole world is facing the COVID-19 pandemic, putting before us an issue that, as Philippe Ariès studied at length,[10] Western society does not want to see: death. Carlo Leget,[11] in his research, realized that a devotional for dying well could not be formulated in the 21st century, at least in his context (the Netherlands) where only 14% say they believe in a personal God. However, there are tasks to tackle at the end of life and these tasks are spiritual.

The Secpal (Spanish Society of Palliative Care) has defined spirituality "as our essential nature, which shapes us as human beings and from which arises our inexhaustible longing for fullness, which aspires to endow our life with meaning, coherence, harmony, and transcendence."[12] This definition is much closer to the experience of spirituality that our contemporaries have. Perhaps many people do not accept a religious framework for their experiences, but they recognize in themselves that "inexhaustible longing for fullness," with its consequences of meaning, coherence, harmony, and transcendence.

Without using these expressions, Leget's intuition is similar and he continues detailing some characteristics of that spiritual path, as he discovered in his research and which I find very similar to my own findings. I will join my intuitions to his and talk about the need to create an interior space and five questions that would act as a contemporary preparation for a "good death."[13]

2.1 The interior space
It is a mental, emotional, and spiritual state in which the person is capable of experiencing thoughts and emotions, without identifying with them or being overwhelmed by them. Putting the concept of interior space at the center of a contemporary formulation of *Ars moriendi* enables people from any spiritual tradition to be included. Leget discusses some attitudes or situations that could facilitate access to that interior space. He chose two that seem especially pertinent to me: spiritual traditions and silence.

As for spiritual traditions, I find that they have many elements that can help us connect with interiority, for example, spiritual or ritual narratives or practices.[14] Silence, for its part, is somehow the same interior space that it leads to. There is nothing to argue with there because it is the place where we meet with ourselves. Silence confronts us, but it also welcomes us and shelters us. People who are at the end of life adopt long spaces of silence, they need them; in that space, many things are processed not only cognitively, but also emotionally and spiritually.[15]

2.2. The five questions
Leget lucidly points out that the *Ars moriendi* of the 15th century were formulated in dualistic and pendulum-like terms: there is only black (demons) or white (angels). In our day, the two poles of the model should not be formulated in terms of "good-evil," but should be considered as more or less general anthropological categories. They must be clear enough to organize our experiences and thoughts, but also open enough

not to limit and close the interpretation of what we experience beforehand.

How could the five end-of-life tasks be rethought so that they can be useful to people in the 21st century? They could be stated as questions, although they are not questions that companions should ask, but rather five points that must be known as important to enable the questions when they arrive, if they arrive.[16]

1. *Who am I and what do I really want?*

The pride and humility that the *Ars moriendi* of the 16th century wielded were moral categories. When we try to reinstate them in anthropological, non-moral categories, we can identify the poles of "oneself" and "others." It is not uncommon for people to understand their story when they are finishing it; it is something quite logical and this makes the "precious time of the end" even more valued. The question our new *Ars Moriendi* becomes: who am I am what do I really want? This allows you to decide how to go through the last stage and with what company. Loved ones are made aware of how the person wants to be accompanied. There are people who have never had the possibility to choose almost anything in their lives; therefore, choosing how and with whom they want to be here and now is always an act of freedom, dignity, and personal sovereignty.[17]

2. *How do I deal with the pain?*

The alternatives in the medieval model were to be patient or impatient. Today, we would put it like this: what do I do with the pain? In the inner stillness we can know when to act – taking painkillers, for example – and when to simply let what is happening happen. The interesting thing is to find peace in this process, in which there are no fixed recipes and in which it is very important to respect one's own feelings.[18]

3. *How do I say goodbye? Do I hold on, cling, or know how to let go?*

In medieval times, the question of detachment was addressed, versus greed and attachment. If clinging desperately to all the good things in life, you cannot die well. The medieval solution was to focus on God. In the new *Ars moriendi*, the question would be formulated like this: How do I say goodbye? Accepting what is happening, letting go of what is good but ends, is a way to leave in peace.

Obviously, this farewell is not improvised - it can be done by those who have trained throughout their lives to release loved ones and loved things. Those who do not have that attitude will need more support, because there is much to elaborate and work on.

4. How do I evaluate my life? Remembrance between forgiveness and guilt
The *Ars moriendi* spoke of hope as a remedy for the temptation of despair. Despair is characterized by the destructive power that the past can have. In this situation, the only way to open up to the future is to let go of the past. Now that my biography is over, how do I remember my life? It is not about cognitive operations, but about a willingness to accept, let go, and re-signify.

Forgiving others and yourself is a way not to change memories, but to give them a new meaning. Although there is no religious thought, guilt is a psychological and spiritual human fact. Asking for forgiveness, forgiving, is very liberating for those who leave and for those who stay.[19]

5. What can I expect?
In the medieval model, there was talk of the opposition between faith and loss of faith. In our days, people seek knowledge based on scientific evidence, but death presents us with a future for which there is no such evidence, at least from the experimental sciences. Faced with death, human beings ask ourselves, what can I expect? The answers are between the poles of believing and knowing. Those who believe in a personal God and their faith is sincere, generally trust and surrender more easily. Atheists or agnostic pass between curiosity, doubt, anguish...[20] Knowing that oneself "matters to the end"[21] feeds that hope, opens spiritual paths that do not necessarily have to do with religious faith but with the fact of knowing oneself loved and worthy of love and loving: a reality that is perceived as defeating death and continuing in another way, although it is not known how.

Thus we have the complete image of a contemporary *Ars moriendi*. It is a framework designed for use at the end of life, but I think that it can bring fulfillment to all people, whatever the vital moment we are going through. Talking about these tasks transforms *Ars Moriendi* into *Ars Vivendi*.

María Marcela Mazzini

Thinking about death certainly helps you live better and be happier.

Translated by Thia Cooper

Notes

1. I do this based on posdoctoral work that I did at the Hospice "San Camilo" between 2014 and 2017. It is located in Olivos, Buenos Aires Province, Argentina: https://www.hospicesancamilo.org.ar/ [29 December 2020]. The study has continued in various ways; today, it is being developed in a research group at my faculty and in fieldwork based on a master's degree that I am doing on cross-cultural spirituality.
2. AAMYCP: The Argentine Association of Medicine and Palliative Care brings together professionals and volunteers of palliative care in Argentina: https://aamycp.com.ar/ [29 December 2020]
3. Carlo Leget, *Art of Living, Art of Dying: Spiritual Care for a Good Death*, London: Jessica Kingsley Publishers, 2017.
4. Modern spirituality does not escape this epochal impulse to find a method for all things, hence the rise of modern devotionals. *Ars moriendi* is nothing more than a devotional that seeks a method of dying well.
5. Ana Luisa Haindl Ugarte, "Ars bene moriendi, el arte de la buena muerte," *Revista Chilena de Estudios Medievales 3* (January-June 2013), 89–108, here 102.
6. These devotionals, up to the fifteenth century, constitute a kind of literary genre in themselves within spiritual literature, but a work of Jean Gerson, Chancellor of the University of Paris (1412-1419), was identified as the *Ars moriendi* at the Council of Constance (1414–1418).
7. See Elisa Ruiz García, "El Ars moriendi: una preparación para el tránsito," in Nicolás Ávila Seoane/Manuel Joaquín Salamanca López/Leonor Zozaya Montes (eds.), *IX Jornadas científicas sobre Documentación: La muerte y sus testimonios escritos*, Madrid: Universidad Complutense de Madrid, 2011, 314–344, here 318.
8. It was from the second chapter of the original version.
9. In fact, the *Ars moriendi* was a true phenomenon of diffusion and reading; the QS version was transformed into the most widespread of xylographic books, especially between 1450 and 1530. See Roger Chartier, "Les arts de mourir, 1450–1600," *Annales Économies, Sociétés*, Civilizations 31.1 (1976), 51–75.
10. See Philippe Ariès, *Historia de la muerte en Occidente: De la Edad Media hasta nuestros días*, traducido por Francisco Carbajo y Richard Perrin, first edition, Barcelona: Acantilado, 2000.
11. He is an ethicist working at Utrecht University in the Netherlands. His specialty is the ethics of care and he has been reflecting on end-of-life issues for years.
12. Manifiesto Secpal-Mallorca, "Por una clínica que acoja la experiencia espiritual del ser humano en el final de su vida," in Enric Benito/Javier Barbero/Mónica Dones, *Espiritualidad en clínica: Una propuesta de evaluación y acompañamiento espiritual en cuidados paliativos*, Buenos Aires: Biblos-Instituto Pallium Latinoamérica, 2015, 285–286, here 285.
13. Today, in the world of palliative care, death is not spoken of as an instant but as a process. The whole process must be good to be able to speak of "good death."
14. Spiritual traditions also connect us with our identity and with childhood habits, with loved people and places that make us feel protected. The Rosary, the stamps, the images are Mary that are in the "house of hope" (of the San Camilo Hospice), give an account of their status as "landmarks of the sacred" important for believers, but equally significant for all the guests and their families.
15. Leget, *Art of Living*, 77–78.

Ars Vivendi: Spirituality for the End of Life in the 21st century

16. Not all of them are necessarily going to be formulated, nor are they going to be formulated in this way, but it is likely that they will appear in the accompaniment of the last weeks or months of life.

17. A guest told me with emotion that until her arrival at the hospice no one had asked her, what would you like to eat now? That detail made her feel loved, cared for, and opened her heart so that she could prepare to live her own life to the end.

18. At the end of life there should be no pain: this is one of the fundamental tasks of palliative care. But also Cicely Saunders, founder of the hospice movement worldwide, spoke of "total pain" or "pain that is difficult to manage" - often these pains have to do with emotional suffering rather than physical pain. It is in these cases that it is especially important to work on the psychological and spiritual dimensions. Experience shows that pain subsides with this approach. See Cicely Saunders, "The Symptomatic Treatment of Incurable Malignant Disease," *Prescribers Journals 4* (1964), 68–73; Cicely Saunders, Velad Conmigo: *Inspiración para una vida en cuidados paliativos*, translated from English by Marisa Martín y Susan Hannam, Barcelona: La Caixa, 2011. [Watch With Me: Inspiration for a Life in Hospice Care.]

19. More than once in the hospice, we have seen how people seem to delay their departure until they can see someone and ask for their forgiveness. Those who remain also heal wounds and can continue their lives healthier when they give or receive forgiveness. In those final dialogues, both things usually happen. On this subject as well, see Harvey Chochinov, *Dignity Therapy: Final Words for Final Days*, New York: Oxford, 2012.

20. We have seen in the hospice that the question of the afterlife is as present as the daily routine of the guests; it still settles in agnostics and atheists, that which we could call a hopeful doubt... "What if you are right?": we heard this question addressed to the believers in the House of Hope more than once.

21. It is a phrase by Cicely Saunders, which gives title to the book of the Hospice Movement of Argentina: See *Movimiento Hospice Argentina, Eres importante hasta el final: Cuidado Hospice*, Buenos Aires: Editorial Claretiana, 2012. [You matter to the end of your life.]

Everything Called In Question: When a Pet is Fatally Ill

TAMAR A. AVRAHAM

After thirteen years together one of our cats was diagnosed with kidney failure. The next four months were nursing and finally accompaniment in death. This raises existential questions: Is Western veterinary practice right when it recommends that incurably ill animals should be put to sleep? How can we decide about the life and death of another creature that cannot unequivocally communicate whether it wants to go on living? What else can we pray for when death is clearly in sight and suffering can no longer be relieved? What happens to the liturgical year in the shadow of illness and death?

The starting-point of this article will be provocative for many people. I am placing the experiences and the ethical questions associated with responding to the illness and death of my cat on the same level as supporting a human being at the end of their life. This has biographical reasons. Cats have shared my life for almost 19 years, first two, at the maximum seven, and now there are still five. Few relationships with human beings have been so long and so deep emotionally. That is why for me the existential confrontation with suffering and death, the crisis in which the existential questions come to the surface, came when Schalgie, the third of the adopted cats, after 13 years of life together, was diagnosed with kidney failure, and the vet gave her at most three to four months to live, which would be a time of continual discomfort and increasing weakness.

The first question didn't come from me, but from the vet. For him it was clear that putting my cat down was the right thing to do. 'When kidney

Everything Called In Question: When a Pet is Fatally Ill

function has declined to such a point, we put them to sleep,' he said, and explained that I didn't have the necessary medical knowledge to judge whether this was the right decision. I began to analyse the logic of this position. Western veterinary medicine works on the assumption that it is legitimate to put to sleep an animal that is incurably ill and in pain. Putting an animal to sleep is the medical response to all cases for which there is no longer any treatment possible other than using more and more powerful drugs. That may have its internal logic, but my criticism starts with the premise: what gives me the right to decide about someone else's life?

Human medicine is prepared at most to recognise the right of someone who is incurably ill to put an end to their own life, possibly by means of a process to be carried out by others, but surely not the autonomous right of others to take this decision. But with an animal, I can't ask it whether it wants to go on living. The vet can assess how it is feeling in terms of health, but that gives no grounds for a conclusion about its desire to live. In the same way, two people with similar symptoms will take different views about whether their life is worth living. If Schalgie had given me a sign that she didn't want to go on living, I might perhaps have had her put to sleep. But she kept coming to me, looking for attention, she would sit on the balcony in the sun, then even on the wall, then on the table, finally, with an effort, on my knee, and finally only on the floor. Until the last day she tried to find these little pleasures, Who was I to decide that that was no definitive argument for going on living? There are countries with a Buddhist culture in which putting animals to sleep is prohibited. So, after all, my position is not so weird.

Naturally I wanted to give Schalgie every possible relief, but there weren't many options. Daily drips would have helped a bit, but on the other hand there would have been the stress of the visits to the vet, which even in better times were torture for her. I wouldn't have managed to put in the drips myself. The animal hospital would definitely not have been an alternative. There she would have been in a cage, surrounded by strangers, when she had never allowed anyone but me to touch her. She would feel that I had betrayed her, and even the little pleasures she still had would be over. So all I could do was to try to keep her spirits up, and as well as dry food giver her as much tinned food as possible, to give her more fluids. By now it didn't matter how healthy the food was; the main thing was that she liked it. Gradually I tried all the brands in the pet shop until there was nothing attractive left, and she only ate tiny mouthfuls.

There was another way I could still make an important difference, being there for her. Being there to react to her calls, to stroke her. One of my jobs is tour guide. I still had an engagement for a tour in Galilee lasting several days, but decided not to stay overnight with the group in the hotel, but to travel back to Jerusalem every evening so I could at least spend the night with Schalgie. The periods I was away from home became shorter and shorter. Sitting at my desk translating, I could see and hear when she needed attention and take breaks accordingly. While I was trying to support Schalgie as much as possible, the Jewish liturgical year went on.

It was a few days before Passover that I received the bad results of the blood test. I had already invited friends for the seder so that we could remember together the exodus experience, and make it real in the present. Schalgie's condition created an acute dissonance between what was set in the calendar and reality. The oppressive atmosphere became more acute as during Passover week I went into the garden underneath the Israel Museum, where in the preceding weeks I had enjoyed nature awakening in the spring. Passover is the spring feast. On the sabbath of the festival week for morning prayer we read the Song of Songs, which also celebrates nature's awakening from its winter dormancy. But spring in Israel is short. Nature hardly reaches its full bloom when the rain ends and there are a few warm days to put a stop to it all. Lots of flowers in the garden had already faded, and the tall grass was beginning to dry. On the other side of the street I could hear the mowers of the city administration, which couldn't get rid of the grass soon enough, to avoid fires. They didn't even wait till after Passover. It would be nine or ten months before there was more fresh green growth and new flowers. Schalgie would not experience it again. The people who were murdered in Sri Lanka in the suicide attacks during the Easter Sunday services would no longer experience it. Sometime it is everyone's last spring. I sat in the grass, and felt only death and decay around me and tears rolled down my face.

There are fifty days between Passover and Shavuot, the Feast of Weeks. Schalkie's energy was stronger than expected, but decreased continuously. Would she experience another Shavuot? Or would she die precisely on Shavuot, the feast of the giving of the Torah, of which I am particularly

Everything Called In Question: When a Pet is Fatally Ill

fond?

Jewish mourning rituals leave a lot of time for taking leave of the dead. After the death of a close relative, you stay at home for a whole week, receive visits of condolence, and can go on talking endlessly about the departed. Up to the thirtieth day, in the case of the death of parents as long as eleven months, in the synagogue service the mourners recite the *kaddish*, a daily remembrance of the dead. But the *halakah* or customary law does not excuse mourners from celebrating the festivals. If a feast day falls in the week of mourning, the period of mourning is reduced and ends before the beginning of the feast day. Personal experiences should not cast a shadow over the community's faith experience. That is the theory. But even in the case of important rabbinic authorities things can turn out differently. I had read that Rabbi Joseph B. Soloveitchik (1903–1993), the founder of modern Orthodox Judaism, recited kaddish for his dead wife not just for thirty days, but for several years. When asked why he acted in violation of the religious rules, he could only reply: 'I can't do anything else.'

Schalgie lived past Shavuot. The month of Tammus was approaching. On the sabbath before every new moon a prayer for a blessed month is said:

> 'May the Holy One, praised be he, renew it over us and over his whole people, the House of Israel, wherever they are, for good things and blessing, for celebration and joy, for healing and comfort, for bread and the sustenance of life, for life and peace, for good news and good happenings, for complete healing and speedy redemption, and let us say Amen.'

Previously this prayer was always a special moment for me. I would concentrate on all the good things I wished for myself in the coming month, and was filled with words of hope. Now it was no longer appropriate. Schalgie was going to die soon. It was not likely that she would even live to the end of this month. What sense did it make any more to pray for her life and her healing? What sense at all does it have to say such a prayer? Each of us will sometime say it for the last time and no longer live to see the answer.

17th Tammus is the beginning of the three weeks of mourning leading up to the commemoration of the destruction of the Temple on 9th Av, a period in which no weddings take place and Orthodox Jews also refrain from parties and music, don't buy new clothes, and as far as possible don't move into new homes. The collective mood of mourning, even though it naturally had a different theological background, suited my situation. I began to read the midrash to the book of Lamentations. This is about the question how God could allow his Temple to be destroyed, Jerusalem to be left rubble and ashes and its inhabitants become desperate with hunger, until finally mothers ate their children. Naturally it gives the answer that this is punishment for our sins. It doesn't hesitate to say to God that he went too far, that he should have had pity.

When the issue is suffering that is not the result of human action, but the result of the fact that human nature is susceptible to illness and death, the question becomes more pressing. Why did God create human beings as condemned to die? This isn't fundamentally changed even by belief in the resurrection, because the question remains: why do human beings only reach eternal life through death?

The 9th Av came. Schalgie was still alive. In the liturgical year the end of the days of fasting and mourning mark the emergence from mourning, the search for new hope. In direct contrast to this, precisely after 9th Av Schalgie's condition worsened. On the Friday she ate and drank nothing at all. I sat at my desk, tried to go on working on a translation, but her voice kept coming from the cushion behind me, and I sat down beside her. Evening came. The sabbath began, the first sabbath after the 9th Av, which called *Nachamu* ('Comfort sabbath', from the line 'Comfort, comfort my people' at the beginning of the prophetic reading from Isaiah 40). This sabbath begins the series of the seven Comfort Sabbaths that lead up to *Rosh Hashanah*, the new year, on which promises from Isaiah are read. Comfort was a very long way away from me.

The heat had eased a little and I opened the door to the balcony. Schalgie went out and sat on the ground, but was to restless to stay there for very long. For the rest of the evening she couldn't sit still. Only when I went to sleep, she also stayed on the armchair near the bed, which in the previous few weeks had become her regular place to spend the night. Around 2.00 a.m. I was awakened by a noise and saw that in an attempt to jump out of the armchair she had fallen over. She pulled herself together once more

Everything Called In Question: When a Pet is Fatally Ill

and climbed, with an effort, over the bed and back to the armchair. I piled up cushions around the armchair so that if she fell again she would have a soft landing. It wasn't long before that happened. This time she couldn't get up again. She lay on her side on the cushions that I had placed there. I sat down decide here and put my hand on her. It was the only thing I could do. Shortly after six, as the sun had just risen, I could no longer feel breathing.

The psalm recitation at morning prayer begins with Psalm 30: 'Weeping may linger for the night, but joy comes with the morning.' Since Schalgie died as dawn broke, I can no longer pray this psalm.

There are many prayers I can no longer say. I can no longer recite prayers automatically. I look at the content of the texts and also for their contradiction with experience, with reality. I find allies in prophets and rabbis who have shot back a 'Why?' at God. The answer, my answer, is one only I can find. It feels its way forward, checks and rejects, takes two steps forward and one back. It will never be complete, but it is authentic.

Translated by Francis McDonagh

Theological Forum

On Hans Küng
(19/03/1928 – 06/04/2021)

JOSÉ OSCAR BEOZZO

On the occasion of Hans Küng's death, the author brings to light Dom Helder Camara's notes about Küng during the Second Vatican Council and recalls Küng's visit to Brazil in October 2007.

Upon receiving this afternoon the news of the death of Hans Küng (19 March 1928, Sursee, Switzerland – 6 April 2021, Germany), I sketched some lines about his life's trajectory that I will share with you. Before the Second Vatican Council, I had already read his book: *Concile et retour à l'unité* (The Council, Reform and Reunion), published in France in 1962.[1] It impacted me greatly. A breath of fresh air, which opened up many horizons for me. The original in German, *Konzil und Wiedervereinigung: Erneuerung als Ruf in der Einheit*, was published by Herder of Freiburg, in 1960. The French publisher reduced to three words the kilometric title of the German edition, a long title, but which expressed well the purpose of the book: 'The Council and the restoration of unity: renewal as a call for unity'.

When I was starting my third year of theology at the Gregorian University in Rome, I heard him for the first time, on 27 October 1962, at Domus Mariae, the large headquarters of Italian Catholic Action, at 481 Aurelia Street, that served as the lodgings for the Brazilian episcopate during the four sessions of the Second Vatican Council (1962–1965). It was a lecture in Spanish for the Brazilian bishops on the History of the Mass. The discussion on Liturgy in the Conciliar Room was just beginning at this time. I returned to hear him again two days later, on the 29th October, at the conference held in the same place on 'The Council and the return to Unity.' I note the reaction to his speech by Dom Helder Camara, at that time the general secretary of the National Conference of the Bishops of Brazil (CNBB):

'In general, when we meet people who have written books, when we hear them talk, they fall short of the published works. In the book, the authors says in an organic, thought out, documented way, what the lecturer presents in a much more messy and superficial way. There are exceptions. Yves Congar, for example (but I'll talk about him another time). Today, I want to refer to Father Hans Kung, who for the second time, has spoken to the Brazilian Bishops, here at Domus Mariae.

Imagine a young priest, 40 years old, strong, friendly, looking warm and human, hair of gold...

Today, he talked to us about the Council and the return to unity. Teaching in Tübingen (the strongest Lutheran center in the world), he asked a Lutheran university professor: If Luther lived today, would he feel it necessary to leave the Catholic Church, to promote reform, or would he try to reform within the Church? The professor, after commenting that Luther did not leave, but was expelled, acknowledged that there is no comparison possible between the Catholic Church in Luther's time and today. And Küng listed the changes that smoothed the paths of union: an even broader, more comprehensive and accurate attitude towards the Holy Scriptures (just think that today is the Day of the Bible; and the effort to spread the Scriptures; and the ever more numerous translations; and their ever more frequent use); liturgical reform, in line with bringing the people ever closer to the celebrated mysteries (communal Masses that are filled with joy); promotion of the laity; [fl.2] the maturity of the Church to admit criticism (non-Catholic observers are stunned by the absolute freedom enjoyed by the Council Fathers. [...]

I ask if the observers present- by number and degree of representation- are proof that the brothers are believing in our sincerity. He thinks so, although he does not forget that 400 years (Protestants) and 900 years (Orthodox) of prejudice, invective, and mutual suspicion cannot be dissipated in a single meeting. (The Pope is now preferring a word that is so much ours. Whoever says meeting, recognizes the need to not stand still, waiting for the whole walk to be done by the other. Pope did not hesitate to acknowledge that we are largely to blame for all that happened.)

I also asked if it wasn't possible and convenient - maintaining the utmost care for Christian families - to open the doors to non-Christians, especially Jews (ancestors who for centuries were our victims) and Muslims (who already have several points in common with us). He did not hesitate. He thinks that, in the case of the Jews, a clear confession of our past sins of anti-Semitism would have an intense effect. [fl 3]

By the way, we are good friends. The third lecture that I was going to give for us (on the episcopacy), I proposed that it be extended to Latin Americans and open to our African brothers, with whom I have been closely united."[2]

Küng also accepted the invitation to come and speak to the students of Colégio Pio Brasileiro, located at the same Via Aurelia, 527, a few steps ahead of Domus Mariae (I don't have the date in my head, but it was still in late October or early November 1962). He created a furor with his presentation and left the house with half of its hair standing on end, as it sparked the imagination and warmed the hearts of hundreds of Brazilian students of theology and philosophy, who dreamed, like him, of a radical change in the life of the Church.

With his death, I lost a person who greatly inspired me at the beginning of the Council and with whom I worked later, unfortunately for a short time, on the Board of Directors of Concilium. May he find God in his deserved rest, as he was caught/trapped[3] by a lot of people within the Church (Ratzinger, John Paul II, Benedict XVI), but he felt welcomed and recognized by Pope Francis, which greatly comforted him in his last years of life and in his illness.

Together with Karl Rahner, SJ, Yves Congar, OP, Marie-Dominique Chenu, OP, Edward Schillebeeckx, OP, he belonged to the first team of theologians who exerted the greatest influence on Vatican II. Perhaps because he was the youngest among them, he was the freest and most daring in this quintet of great Catholic theologians.

In the footnote I wrote about his first lecture at Domus Mariae, I placed the impressions of Dom Helder Camara, reproduced above.[4] I then gleaned from his Circular Letters, other comments of Dom Helder, with respect to Hans Küng. He doesn't hide his enthusiasm for the young Swiss theologian. Here are some examples:

'In the afternoon there was a splendid lecture here by Hans Küng, professor at the University of Tübingen (Germany), on the history of the Mass. [...] He has the German depth and the Austrian finesse."[5]

'Today, Hans Küng (priest) – whose book was presented by the dear A.C. [Catholic Action], in one of the first bulletins of the Council, which I will soon send, with comments – returns to give us a lecture at Domus Mariae. He is charming! We will continue to push for the Council."[6]

In the third session of the Council (1964), Dom Helder offered a new light commentary on Hans Küng, revealing that the admiration was reciprocal:

"Upon arriving at Domus, at the end of Hans Küng's lecture, with whom I stayed, afterwards, until 11:30pm (I consider him the most audacious of our theologians when he writes and even more so when he speaks; he calls me a prophet)."[7]

From 20-27 October 2007, Hans Küng came to Brazil and staged a veritable marathon of lectures at the country's prestigious universities in Rio Grande do Sul, Paraná, Distrito Federal, Rio de Janeiro and Minas Gerais, where he received the Title of Doctor Honoris Causa from the Federal University of Juiz de Fora. We met at his lecture at Candido Mendes University in Rio Janeiro, attended by more than 500 people, and soon after, at the dinner offered to him by the Dean Dr. Candido Mendes. It was our farewell. The organizer of the event, Luiz Alberto Gomez de Souza, asked him: What could the ethical tradition that emerged from the Latin American and Caribbean experience add to Hans Küng's incessant search for a global ethics and for a dialogue between religions in search of world peace? And his answer was: "The angle from which there can be a new contribution is that of the cry of the poor, the urgency of the questions of justice and equality."

Notes

1. Paris: Editions du Cerf, collection "Unam Sanctam," no 36.
2. Dom Helder Camara, *Circulares conciliares,* vol. 1/tomo I (13 December 1962 to March 1964), collected by Luiz Carlos Luz Marques and Roberto de Araújo Faria, Recife: Editora CEP e Instituto Dom Helder Camara, 2009, 41–42. The letters are referred to as Helder Circulars (HC), followed by their number and the date they were written.
3. Translator's note: *apanhar* can be used in the sense of being caught/ taken in/ beaten/ trapped.
4. José Oscar Beozzo, *A Igreja do Brasil no Concílio Vaticano II: 1959–1965*, São Paulo: Paulinas/Rio de Janeiro: UCAM/Petrópolis: CAAL/Sobral: UVA, 2005, p.196, n 4.
5. HC 13, 26 and 27-10-1962, 36–37.
6. HC 14, 28-10-62, 40.
7. Dom Helder Camara, *Circulares conciliares,* vol. I/tomo II (from 12 September to 22/23 November 1964) org. Luiz Carlos Luz Marques e Roberto de Araújo Faria, Recife: Editora CEP e Instituto Dom Helder Camara, 2009, HC 56, 28/29-10-64, 218.

The Catholic Bishops of Canada Apologize to the Indigenous Peoples of the Land

MICHEL ANDRAOS

After many years of hesitation and tensions within the Canadian Catholic Church about offering an apology to the Indigenous peoples, the Conference of Catholic Bishop has finally been morally forced to take this step. This overdue apology, done in a spirit of humility and brokenness, could potentially open a new path towards a more reconciled future.

'We, the Catholic Bishops of Canada, gathered in Plenary this week, take this opportunity to affirm to you, the Indigenous Peoples of this land, that we acknowledge the suffering experienced in Canada's Indian Residential Schools. Many Catholic religious communities and dioceses participated in this system, which led to the suppression of Indigenous languages, culture and spirituality, failing to respect the rich history, traditions and wisdom of Indigenous Peoples. We acknowledge the grave abuses that were committed by some members of our Catholic community; physical, psycho-logical, emotional, spiritual, cultural, and sexual. We also sorrowfully acknowledge the historical and ongoing trauma and the legacy of suffering and challenges faced by Indigenous Peoples that continue to this day. Along with those Catholic entities which were directly involved in the operation of the schools and which have already offered their own heartfelt apologies, we, the Catholic Bishops of Canada, express our profound remorse and apologize unequivocally.'[1]

The Catholic Bishops of Canada Apologize to the Indigenous Peoples

The shocking news last May and June about the discovery of the unmarked graves of several hundred children who died in what was called Indian Residential Schools created outrage among many Indigenous communities, survivors of the schools, and other Canadians. Vigils were held across the country to show solidarity with the survivors, their families, and communities, and all the Indigenous peoples of Canada. Children's shoes, teddy bears, and flowers were left on the doorsteps of churches and cathedrals, and in public squares. Media reports of these powerful symbolic gestures were seen around the world.

In the following weeks, protests also took place across the country. Several churches, many of which are located on Indigenous reserves, were set on fire and vandalized, acts that angered the Indigenous communities. Official celebrations of Canada Day on July 1st, which marked the founding of Canada by the British in 1867, were cancelled. Statues of political figures representing Canada's colonial era were toppled, including those of Queen Victoria and Queen Elizabeth II in the city of Winnipeg. In some places, street signs that carried names of founding figures of Canadian history were vandalized. A feeling of shame and guilt dominated the mood of the country.

The voices of these children, and the thousands of others who suffered a similar fate, were heard in the conscience of many Canadians. Elder Willard Pine of Garden River First Nation articulates this well:

> With the 215 graves discovered at the Kamloops Residential School and the 751 graves at the Marieval Residential School in Saskatchewan, with many others to come, the little spirits are finally able to tell their story. Although suppressed for many years, these spirits are now crying out for justice and dignity like never before. This is the time of the little spirits. The image across the country of the shoes and teddy bears is a symbol of these children walking for justice, for the need to tell their stories that in life they were denied.

Elder Willard adds, "we should now be listening to all Indigenous children, as every child matters."[2]

Indeed, it is the voices of these children that Canadians are hearing today. And it is these voices and the public's outrage that pressured the

Catholic Bishops of Canada to issue an official apology on September 24, 2021. It is an apology that the survivors of residential schools and all Indigenous peoples of Canada have been expecting, yet were denied for many years.

Over the past several years, many Catholic bishops in Canada apologized to the survivors of the residential schools and, in the name of their diocese, apologized to Indigenous peoples. Other Canadian churches and religious orders, those who were directly responsible for running residential schools, have also repeatedly issued apologies over the last three decades. This summer, several Catholic bishops made genuine statements of sympathy and solidarity in response to the discovery of the unmarked graves and restated their commitment to work for healing and reconciliation. But, there were also some statements made by leading bishops that were ill-prepared and not well received, which added to the public's outrage, especially among the Catholic laity.[3] Some lay groups collected signatures and declared that they would leave the Catholic Church if the bishops did not collectively make an official apology and respond to the demands of the Calls to Action of the Truth and Reconciliation Commission of Canada (TRC).[4]

Comprehending the depth of the pain, including the multigenerational trauma created by the residential schools, and the damage done to entire generations and communities of Indigenous peoples are still unfolding. This work continues to unfold despite the publicly available witness reports, research, many studies, and the Final Report of the TRC.5 What remains challenging to many Canadians is understanding the magnitude of the destruction to the way of life of Indigenous peoples, a process that gradually took place since the beginning of colonization. This eventually led to the creation of residential schools in the middle of the 19th century. Most of the main churches in Canada have been involved in this process and share responsibility for its consequences. The residential schools were intended to be the final chapter of colonization but did not achieve the intended results of the Canadian state and churches. The survivors and their descendants are now demanding their rights, dignity, and humanity.

The discovery of the unmarked graves did not bring any new information to the Canadian public. The presence of graves on the grounds of the residential schools has been known for many years. Volume 4 of

The Catholic Bishops of Canada Apologize to the Indigenous Peoples

the *Final Report of the Truth and Reconciliation of Canada*, entitled 'Canada's Residential Schools: Missing Children and Unmarked Burials', is dedicated to this topic and the information is publicly available.[6] A Working Group on Missing Children and Unmarked Burials was created in 2007 as part of the settlement agreement that led to the creation of the TRC. The task of the Working Group was to investigate: "1) Who and how many residential school students died? 2) What did residential school students die from? 3) Where are the residential school students buried? 4) Who were the residential school students who went missing?"[7] The findings of the TRC on these questions were published in 2015 as part of the Final Report. The recent discovery of the graves, however, provided more concrete information concerning this tragic chapter in the history of residential schools. Canadians began to consciously hear the voices of the children cry out from the ground.

The official apology issued on September 24, 2021, had been previously avoided by the Canadian Catholic Church. In the apology, the Catholic bishops spoke in one voice on behalf of the whole Canadian Catholic Church and apologized to the Indigenous peoples of the country. Before this apology was issued, they insisted that "The Catholic community in Canada has a decentralized structure. Each Diocesan Bishop is autonomous in his diocese and, although relating to the Canadian Conference of Catholic Bishops, is not accountable to it."[8]

Decentralization was, therefore, used as a justification for the Conference of Catholic Bishops to avoid speaking on behalf of the whole Canadian Catholic Church to apologize for what happened at the residential schools and the violence used against Indigenous peoples. The official apology, however, assumes this collective responsibility. The Indigenous peoples of Canada, along with many other Canadians, have been continually frustrated because no responsibility was taken for the collective actions of the Catholic Church. The Calls to Action of the TRC further demanded that the Pope come to Canada and offer an apology to the survivors of the residential schools on behalf of the Catholic Church of Canada. Finally, and humbly, the bishops spoke in one voice: "We, the Catholic Bishops of Canada, gathered in Plenary this week [...] express our profound remorse and apologize unequivocally." In three well-articulated and concise paragraphs, the apology addresses some of the key demands of the Calls to

Action of the TRC and the Indigenous peoples of Canada. The text reflects a genuine sense of remorse and humility. The opening paragraph, cited at the beginning of this article, expresses this message well.

Another key point of this statement of apology is the commitment of the Canadian Catholic Church to the long-term processes of healing and reconciliation, pledging to raise funds for supporting such initiatives in all regions. This remains an unfulfilled promise from previous years. The bishops humbly ask the Indigenous peoples to accompany them on the path of listening and learning, and commit to the "memorialization of those buried in the unmarked graves." They support the visit to the Vatican by an Indigenous delegation to meet with Pope Francis in December of 2021. Furthermore, a request for Pope Francis to come to Canada and offer an apology, which many Canadian bishops have been opposing since 2015, is now considered for discussion. From the tone of the apology, the Canadian bishops seem to be willing to support this visit.

The road ahead remains, however, long. The apology is undoubtedly a milestone that opens a new horizon of hope for the work of more truth-finding about the past, healing, and reconciliation.[9] After many years and getting stuck in the technicalities about who should speak for the Catholic Church of Canada, the bishops seem to have moved beyond that. The apology is a breakthrough for the Catholic bishops and Church of Canada. There will be certainly mixed reactions to this apology from both Indigenous and non-Indigenous people. Some may say it is already too late, that too much damage has been done. Perhaps, the reluctance of the bishops to issue a collective apology has brought further hurt and hardened the position of Indigenous peoples and Canadians towards the Catholic Church. The relationship remains strained between survivors of residential schools, many Indigenous peoples, and the Canadian churches, especially the Catholic Church. There is certainly an accumulated feeling of lack of credibility towards the institutional churches. Indigenous peoples have indeed lost a sense of trust because of repeatedly broken promises. Whether this new official apology will be accepted and will open a new chapter in the relationship with the Catholic Church has yet to be seen. Its acceptance will largely depend on the future actions of the Catholic bishops and diocesan churches over the coming months and years, and on their dedication to the commitments that have been made. But the apology is, nevertheless, a step in the right direction.

The Faculty of Theology at Saint Paul University, the institution where I work, has, in the past year, made significant advancements for a continued and deeper dialogue with Indigenous peoples. We have already been working in the spirit of this recent apology. Our newly founded "Centre for the Churches, Truth, and Reconciliation with Indigenous Peoples" has launched several initiatives for the theological education of our students. Students are taught by Indigenous Elders on reconciliation, Indigenous spirituality and its significance to the whole church. Several members of our Faculty of Theology will soon be meeting to learn from Catholic Indigenous Elders about their spirituality and how to walk together on the road towards reconciliation. As educators, we are committed to the formation of our students by taking up our responsibility to be formed through a dialogue with Indigenous peoples. This new direction, I believe, is a crucial responsibility of all theological schools in Canada. There is a need to rethink Christianity from the perspective of the encounter with the Indigenous peoples of this land. We need to move away from the colonial theological education models of the past. Contributing to the work of decolonizing the churches is a major theological task for the future generation of theologians, if we are to take this apology seriously.

Notes

1. Statement of Apology by the Catholic Bishops of Canada to the Indigenous Peoples of this Land, issued on September 24, 2021. For this and further quotes from the statement, see https://www.cccb.ca/letter/statement-of-apology-by-the-catholic-bishops-of-canada-to-the-indigenous-peoples-of-this-land/ [29 September 2021].
2. Quotes used by Elizabeth Kingston in her paper for the course entitled "Churches and Reconciliation with Indigenous Peoples," Saint Paul University, Ottawa, June 12–19, 2021. I am grateful to Elder Willard Pine of Garden River First Nation, a direct descendant of Chief Shingwauk, for granting us permission to use this quote. Elder Willard is also the Indigenous Spiritual Advisor to the Anglican Archbishop of the Algoma Diocese.
3. For comments on the crisis of leadership in the Catholic Church of Canada this summer, see Michael W. Higgins, "The Wrong Men: Canada's Crisis of Catholic Leadership," La Croix International, 31 July 2021, https://international.la-croix.com/news/religion/the-wrong-men/14736 [29 September 2021].
4. The TRC reports and Calls to Action are available at: https://nctr.ca/records/reports/#trc-reports [29 September 2021].
5. A bibliography of a large amount of literature and resources on this topic by Indigenous and non-Indigenous authors is available on the website of the National Centre for Truth and Reconciliation; https://archives.nctr.ca/Books?page=1&sort=alphabetic&sortDir=asc&listLimit=10 [29 September 2021].

6. *Canada's Residential Schools: Missing Children and Unmarked Burials,* The Final Report of the Truth and Reconciliation Commission of Canada, vol. 4, 2015, available at: https://ehprnh2mwo3.exactdn.com/wp-content/uploads/2021/01/Volume_4_Missing_Children_English_Web.pdf [29 September 2021].

7. *Canada's Residential Schools: Missing Children and Unmarked Burials,* 5.

8. See the section of the Catholic Bishops Conference webpage on Indian Residential Schools and the TRC at: https://www.cccb.ca/indigenous-peoples/indian-residential-schools-and-trc/ [29 September 2021].

9. For a discussion on the long-term theological and pastoral challenges of reconciliation with the Indigenous peoples of Canada, see the articles in the previous issue of Concilium (no. 4, 2019) on "Christianities and Indigenous Peoples," edited by Michel Andraos, Bernardeth Caero Bustillos, and Geraldo De Mori; for example Harry Lafond, "The Church and the Indigenous Peoples of Canada: A Cree Vision of the Church, and My Experience as a Cree Catholic," 50–58, and Michel Andraos, "Long-Term Theological and Pastoral Challenges for Decolonizing the Relation with Indigenous Peoples: A Reflection from Canada," 97–106.

The Synodal Path in Germany: An Interim Report at Half-Time

STEFAN ORTH

Since the abuse scandal a series of topics related to reform of the Catholic Church have been more intensively discussed in Germany. In the 'Synodal Path' bishops and laity together are trying to reach binding commitments that can be translated into proposals for reform. For some of these it will be the universal Church that has to decide.

In the beginning was the abuse scandal. As in other local churches, the discussions about reform in the Catholic Church have become more vigorous since the depressing occurrences of sexual violence on the part of priests and religious and also the cover-up of these by the Church authorities became public.

As early as 2010, as the events in Germany became known to the wider public, the then president of the German Bishops Conference (DBK), the archbishop of Freiburg, Robert Zollitsch, was put under so much pressure that he promoted a 'dialogue process' to discuss the systemic causes of abuse in the Catholic Church. What happened to it? It was first officially downgraded to a 'conversation process' and then, apart from a more open exchange between bishops and representatives of the laity and a series of improvements in the atmosphere, produced little in the way of solid results.

In March 2013 the Association of German Dioceses commissioned a research project on the topic of 'Sexual Abuse of Minors by Catholic Priests, Deacons and Male Religious in the territory of the German Bishops Conference'. The final report, known as the MHG Study, was presented at the Autumn plenary assembly of the German Bishops Conference on 25 September 2018. It detailed the cases since the Second World War - at least – 3,667 affected and 1,670 accused.[1] The indignation in the general public, but also in the Catholic public, after the publication of the study was so great that the Central Committee of German Catholics (ZdK), the highest lay body in German Catholicism, asked the bishops to make an urgent start on practical reforms. A synod governed by canon law seemed too restrictive for the questions to be dealt with, and as a result it was decided to begin a so-called 'synodal path' in which there could be more open discussions, but which also – and this was important for the bishops – could work on binding decisions. Among what the MHG Study had called painful points, a number were chosen to be more intensively dealt with in 'forums'; these were forms of priestly life, power structures in the Church and sexual morality. The ZdK for its part, and especially the female members of diocesan councils, delegates of Catholic associations and prominent individuals, pressed for a fourth forum on the role of women in the Church. The precise titles of the working groups are: 'Power and the Distribution of Authority in the Church', 'Shared Participation and Ownership in Mission', 'Priestly Existence Today', 'Women in Service Roles and Offices in the Church' and 'Life in Successful Relationships – Living Love in Sexuality and Partnership'.[2]

The opening event took place in January 2020 with the just over 230 synod members, including all bishops and auxiliary bishops, and delegates nominated by the DBK and ZdK. The event was held in and around Frankfurt cathedral. Relatively soon afterwards the Corona pandemic upset the timetable for the reforms. The individual forums had difficulty in getting organised and until spring 2021 the work largely took place in video conferences. Instead of the second plenary assembly planned for September 2020, it nevertheless proved possible to hold five regional conferences. At the beginning of February 2021 work was going on completely virtually in so-called hearings on the positions developed to date in the various forums and sub-groups. It must be said that this went so well that there seems no reason why the second plenary session, with consultation on the first draft decisions should not take place in Autumn 2021 in any case – if necessary as a video conference with the relevant tools for voting.[3] After some delay, those affected by sexual violence are now to be more closely involved in the Synodal Path. Thomas Sternberg, as ZdK president part of the four-member steering committee, recalled in this connection that in the Synodal Path 'old reform proposals that have been left in the freezer since the 1970s' are finally being discussed again because of the abuse scandal.

Essentially it has been demonstrated from the beginning the deliberations have no automatic guarantee of success. On the other hand the majorities are clear and it is by no means the case that there is a simple opposition between bishops and laity. An estimated 90% or more support the process in principle, whereas notably the Cologne cardinal Rainer Maria Woelki has on many occasions made his reservations clear. Together with a few other bishops and their nominees to the assembly they form a vocal minority who defend the status quo on the Catholic Church's 'hot topics', such as obligatory celibacy, the blessing of same-sex partnerships and the ordination of women. Similarly not a few bishops also tend to fear changes, but on the other hand know that they have to stay in dialogue with their faithful, who for the most part want changes. That is at any rate true of the delegates and the Church groups and bodies they represent, but now largely also of the core communities, whether churchgoers or simply involved out of interest. It is, however, unclear which reform proposals will secure the two-thirds majority, not only in the plenary assembly but also among the bishops, that is required by the rules of the Synodal Way for them to become binding decisions.

In the end the conservative minority also weakened itself. Cardinal Woelki was under massive pressure for concealing a report on how abusers were treated in the archdiocese of Cologne. His auxiliary bishop, Dominikus Schwaderlapp, who had left the sexual morality forum because he felt that Church teaching was not sufficiently defended, was removed from office after allegations of a cover-up, and submitted his resignation to the Pope. On the other side, after Cardinal Reinhard Marx decided not to stand for a further term as president of the bishops conference, Thomas Sternberg also announced that he would not be available for a further period as president of the central committee of Catholic laity. These two men were among the architects of the Synodal Path.

It is therefore completely impossible to predict what the result of the Synodal Path may be. It is scheduled to end provisionally in summer 2022, that is, shortly before the opening of the Synod of Bishops on 'synodality'. Practical decisions are planned. Everything that falls within the authority of the local Church in canon law is to be implemented immediately. In the case of other decisions Roman approval will be needed. Ultimately there will be a series of demands that affect the universal Church as a whole and can only be given a response at that level – for example, the ordination of women as priests or even just deacons. The new president of the German Bishops Conference, Bishop Georg Batzing of Limburg, who regards the Synodal Path as very important, has agreed to present such proposals in Rome.

In practice the four forums will each have to produce several short draft resolutions that will then be put to a vote. The first texts all came from the forum dealing with power and concerned diocesan finances, preaching by lay people and an Ombudsman's office for dealing with abuse of power. The four sub-groups of the forum on forms of priestly life worked on reforms of training for the priesthood, celibacy (and how it can be lived), and also how to deal with the increasing isolation of elderly priests.

The sub-groups of the forum on the role of women in the Church are focusing on how women can be better involved in decisions within the general parameters of canon law, how greater gender justice can be can be brought about in the Church as a matter of principle, and whether the conditions for access to ordination can be changed. Especially in the forum on sexual morality, there have been fierce clashes between supporters and opponents of reform. A first text could only be produced as a synopsis in which passages with opposing views on particular themes were printed in parallel columns.

All the recommendations for action of each of the four forums are to have an introductory theological text of up to 40 pages explaining the principles underlying the recommendations. At the end of the first year of discussions within the Synodal Path it has become clear that the language used in these texts will be a decisive factor in the success of the documents. On the one hand they must have a broad appeal and therefore also as far as possible be written in accessible language, and on the other the arguments must be completely watertight.

It is clear to all, whether reformers or conservatives, that much is at stake for the universal Church. This applies most recently after the unusual procedure adopted by Pope Francis in summer 2019, before the beginning of the Synodal Path, when he wrote a letter 'to the pilgrim People of God in Germany' that contained a number of phrases in which the critics felt confirmed. Equally the initiators of the Pope's remarks could count this as support for their cause.[4]

Many other local Churches have indicated their interest in the next stages of the Synodal Path, and a good few have sent observers.[5] And not least a series of statements from the Vatican Curia give the impression of being direct replies to the debates in the Synodal Path, for example the Responsum ('reply') of the Congregation for the Doctrine of the Faith in the middle of March on the blessing of same-sex partnerships.

The delegates, who include a number of celebrated German professors of theology, are well aware that for this very reason solid theological arguments have to be presented in order to lobby in the universal Church for the positions of the Church in Germany. The criticism of the official observer Czeslaw Kozon, bishop of Copenhagen, could not have been clearer when he said that the Synodal Path's response to the abuse problem was to have discussions on structures that were a distraction from the real issue.

This is only one of the reasons for which, as well as a preface, work is under way on a statement of principles – perhaps to go as an insert before the individual texts – that clarifies specific issues that affect the various areas: How should we read the bible? How far can theological positions be justified by tradition? How should we understand the relationship between theology and the magisterium, and between the local Church and the universal Church? Also helpful would be an explanation of the engagement with the 'signs of the times' called for by the Second Vatican Council, and a definition of the role the 'sense of the faithful' has on all issues.

A good many people are indicating that in Francis' pontificate, since he has declared synodality to be an essential element of the Catholic Church, there is a window of opportunity for reforms. We want to use this, in a structured way. Whether this can succeed, however, is still an open question. Among the laity at least there is great impatience. It is good that Pope Francis has stressed the importance of synodal deliberations for the reform of the Catholic Church by calling for the preparations for the next

Stefan Orth

synod of bishops to take place in all dioceses throughout the world.

Translated by Francis McDonagh

Notes

1. Research Project 'Sexueller Missbrauch an Minderjährigen durch katholische Priester, Diakone und männliche Ordensangehörige im Bereich der Deutschen Bischofskonferenz', Mannheim, Heidelberg and Gießen, 24 September 2018. The full text of the study can be found at: https://www.dbk.de/fileadmin/redaktion/diverse_downloads/dossiers_2018/MHG-Studie-gesamt.pdf [Accessed 31/10/2021]. A summary is available at: https://www.dbk.de/fileadmin/redaktion/diverse_downloads/dossiers_2018/MHG-Studie-Endbericht-Zusammenfassung.pdf [Accessed 31/10/2021].
2. See the English version of the Synodal Path website:: https://www.synodalerweg.de/english [Accessed 31/10/2021].
3. In the end the second plenary assembly was an in-person event, held in Frankfurt am Main from 30 September to 2 October 2021.
4. An English text of the Pope's letter can be found here:
https://www.plenarycouncil.catholic.org.au/wp-content/uploads/2019/08/LETTER-OF-THE-HOLY-FATHER-FRANCIS-to-Church-in-Germany.pdf (Accessed 01/11/2021].
5. They included France, Belgium, Poland Chechnya, Switzerland, Denmark, Austria and Luxembourg.

Contributors

PROF. DR. DOUGLAS J. DAVIES is a professor in the study of religion and Director of the Centre for Death and Life Studies, Durham University, trained in anthropology and theology. He has published numerous monographs in death studies. He holds Oxford's higher Doctor of Letters degree and an honorary S.T.D from Uppsala. Anglican Priest. Fellow of the Academy of Social Sciences, and of the British Academy.
Address: Department of Theology and Religion, University of Durham, Abbey House, Palace Green, Durham DH1 3RS, UK
Email: douglas.davies@durham.ac.uk

DR DIETMAR METH was born in 1940 and was professor of moral theology in Fribourg, Switzerland (1974-1981) and from 1981 to 2008 professor of theological ethics and social ethics in Tübingen. From 1991 to 2001 he set up and directed the International Centre for 'Ethics in the Sciences' at the University of Tübingen. Since 2009 he has been a fellow of the Max Weber Kolleg of the University of Erfurt. His autobiography, Nicht einverstanden: Erfahrungen eines Laientheologen in Kirche und Gesellschaft, was published in 2020.
Address: Bergstrasse 141 C, D-44791 Bochum, Germany
Email: dietmar.mieth@uni-tuebingen.de

KRIS H.K. CHONG (PhD, Fuller Theological Seminary; MPhil, Cambridge University) teaches at Baptist Theological Seminary, Singapore. Her research interests are: theology and film, religion and popular culture, and Chinese and Japanese literature. A columnist for Singapore's Chinese newspapers, Chong's other work includes Transcendence and Spirituality in Chinese Cinema: A Theological Exploration (Routledge, 2020), and a collection of Chinese prose (forthcoming).
Address: Baptist Theological Seminary, Singapore, 1023 Upper Seran-

Contributors

goon Rd, Singapore 534761, Republic of Singapore
Email: kris.chong@bts.org.sg

ANDREA VICINI, SJ, MD, PhD, and STD, is Michael P. Walsh Professor of Bioethics in the Theology Department at Boston College. His research interests and publications include theological bioethics, global public health, new biotechnologies, environmental issues, and fundamental theological ethics.
Address: Boston College. Theology Department, 140 Commonwealth Avenue, Chestnut Hill, MA 02467, USA
Email: andrea.vicini@bc.edu

ALEXANDRE A. MARTINS is a Brazilian theologian and bioethicist. He is assistant professor at the Theology Department and the College of Nursing at Marquette University (Wisconsin, USA). He received a PhD in theological ethics/bioethics from Marquette University and developed post-doctorate research at the Human Rights Center of the University of Coimbra, Portugal. He has vast international experience serving in global health. He is currently the Regional Coordinator for Latin American and the Caribbean of Catholic Theological Ethics in the World Church (CTEWC). His several books include The Cry of the Poor: Liberation Ethics and Justice in Health Care (Lexington Books, 2020).
Address: 1217 W. Wisconsin Ave., Milwaukee, WI 53233, USA
Email: alexandre.martins@marquette.edu

PROFESSOR DR JEAN-PIERRE WILS (born 1957) studied philosophy and Catholic theology in Leuven (Belgium) and Tübingen (Germany). He held a Heisenberg scholarship from the German Research Foundation from 1992 to 1995, and is a member of German PEN. His recent publications include Das Nachleben der Toten: Philosophie auf der Grenze (Mentis Verlag, 2019), Sich den Tod geben: Suizid als letzte Emanzipation? (Hirzel, 2021).
Address: Stiftsgasse 1, NL-47559 Kranenburg, Netherlands
Email: j.p.wils@ftr.ru.nl

ERIC MARCELO O. GENILO SJ is an ordained minister and a

Contributors

member of the Philippine Province of the Society of Jesus. He earned his licentiate and doctoral degrees at the former Weston Jesuit School of Theology in Cambridge, Massachusetts (currently the School of Theology and Ministry of Boston College). He is a professor at Loyola School of Theology in the Ateneo de Manila University where he teaches courses in moral theology. He is also a formator of diocesan seminarians at the San Jose Seminary in Quezon City, Philippines.
Address: Loyola School of Theology, Ateneo de Manila University, Loyola Heights, 1108 Quezon City, Philippines, Mail: P.O. Box 240, U.P. Post Office, 1144 Quezon City, Philippines
Email: egenilo@hotmail.com

ABDULAZIZ SACHEDINA, PhD, is Professor and Endowed IIIT Chair in Islamic Studies at George Mason University in Fairfax, Virginia. His research focuses on the field of Islamic law, ethics, and theology (Sunni and Shiite), especially social and political ethics, including interfaith and intrafaith relations, Islamic biomedical ethics, and Islam and human rights. Dr. Sachedina's publications include Islamic Biomedical Ethics: Theory and Application, Islam and the Challenge of Human Rights (Oxford University Press, 2009), in addition to numerous articles in academic journals.
Address: 4428 George Mason Blvd, Fairfax, VA 22030, USA
Email: asachedi@gmu.edu

MARÍA MARCELA MAZZINI has a doctorate in Theology from the Catholic University of Argentina and is the Chair of Spiritual Theology and is Coordinator of the Institute of Theological Research at the Faculty of Theology (UCA), where she participates in a research group on the topic of spirituality at the end of life. She is a teacher in the Master's in Palliative Care at the Pallium Foundation, Argentina.
Address: 33 Orientales 424 (1643) Beccar. Provincia de Buenos Aires. Argentina
Email: mmazzini@uca.edu.ar

TAMAR A. AVRAHAM was born in 1965. She has an MA in theology, additional studies in Judaism, Islamic studies and comparative religion.

Contributors

She is a tour guide in Israel and translates academic theology. She lives in Jerusalem.
Address: c/o Margareta Gruber, Philosophisch-Theologische Hochschule Vallendar, Pallottistrasse 3, 56179 Vallendar, Germany
Email: tamar-av@013.net

FATHER JOSÉ OSCAR BEOZZO is vicar of the São Benedito Parish, in Lins, SP, a doctor in social history from USP, and the general coordinator of CESEEP–The Ecumenical Center for Evangelization and Popular Education Services.
Address: Rua Dr. Mário Vicente 1108 - Fundos, Vila Dom Pedro I – Ipiranga, São Paulo SP, 04270-001, Brasil
Email: jbeozzo@terra.com.br

MICHEL ANDRAOS is the dean of the Faculty of Theology at Saint Paul University in Ottawa, Canada. His main areas of teaching and research include intercultural theology, theologies of interreligious dialogue, and religion and culture. The focus of his current research and engagement is the churches and reconciliation with Indigenous Peoples and theological dialogue with Indigenous resurgences and spiritualities.
Address: Faculty of Theology, Saint Paul University, 223 Main Street, Ottawa, Ontario K1S 1C4, Canada
Email: mandraos@ustpaul.ca

STEFAN ORTH has a doctorate in theology, was born in 1968 and is deputy chief editor of the Catholic monthly *Herder Korrespondenz: Monatsheft für Gesellschaft und Religion*. He studied Catholic theology in Freiburg, Paris und Münster, and received his doctoral degree in 1998. He has been an editor of Herder Korrespondenz since 1998 and deputy chief editor since 2014.
Address: Redaktion Herder-Korrespondenz, Hermann-Herder-Straße 4, D-79104 Freiburg, Germany
Email: orth@herder.de

CONCILIUM
International Journal of Theology

FOUNDERS
Antoine van den Boogaard; Paul Brand; Yves Congar, OP; Hans Küng; Johann Baptist Metz; Karl Rahner, SJ; Edward Schillebeeckx

BOARD OF DIRECTORS
President: Thierry-Marie Courau OP
Vice-Presidents: Susan Abraham, Carlos Mendoza-Álvarez OP, Stefanie Knauss, Daniel Franklin Pilario CM

BOARD OF EDITORS
Susan Abraham, Los Angeles (USA)
Michel Andraos, Chicago (USA)
Antony John Baptist, Bangalore (India)
Michelle Becka, Würzburg (Germany)
Sharon A. Bong, Selangor (Malaysia)
Bernadeth Caero Bustillos, Osnabrück (Germany)
Catherine Cornille, Boston (USA)
Thierry-Marie Courau OP, Paris (France)
Geraldo Luiz De Mori SJ, Belo Horizonte (Brazil)
Margareta Gruber OSF, Vallendar (Germany)
Stan Chu Ilo, Chicago (USA)
Gustáv Kovacs, Pecs (Hungary)
Huang Po-Ho, Tainan (Taiwan)
Stefanie Knauss, Villanova (USA)
Carlos Mendoza-Álvarez OP, Ciudad de México (Mexico)
Esther Mombo, Limuru (Kenya)
Gianluca Montaldi FN, Brescia (Italy)
Daniel Franklin Pilario CM, Quezon City (Philippines)
Carlos Schickendantz, Santiago (Chile)
Stephan van Erp OP, Leuven (Belgium)

PUBLISHERS
SCM Press (London, UK)
Matthias-Grünewald Verlag (Ostfildern, Germany)
Editrice Queriniana (Brescia, Italy)
Editorial Verbo Divino (Estella, Spain)
EditoraVozes (Petropolis, Brazil)

Concilium Secretariat:
Couvent de l'Annonciation
222 rue du Faubourg Saint-Honoré
75008 – Paris (France)
secretariat.concilium@gmail.com
Executive secretary: Gianluca Montaldi FN

http://www.concilium.in

Concilium Subscription Information

February **2022/1:** *New Developments in Theology in Asia*

April **2022/2**: *Covid-19: Beyond the Anthropocene?*

July **2022/3:** *Contextual Biblical Interpretation*

October **2022/4:** *Theology of Animals*

December **2022/5**: *Hospitality and Friendship Today*

New subscribers: to receive the next five issues of Concilium please copy this form, complete it in block capitals and send it with your payment to the address below. Alternatively subscribe online at www.conciliumjournal.co.uk

Please enter my annual subscription for Concilium starting with issue 2021/2.

Individuals
____ £52 UK
____ £75 overseas and (Euro €92, US $110)

Institutions
____ £75 UK
____ £95 overseas and (Euro €120, US $145)

Postage included – airmail for overseas subscribers

Payment Details:
Payment can be made by cheque or credit card.
a. I enclose a cheque for £/$/€ ____ Payable to Hymns Ancient and Modern Ltd
b. To pay by Visa/Mastercard please contact us on +44(0)1603 785911 or go to www.conciliumjournal.co.uk

Contact Details:
Name ....
Address ....
....
Telephone .... E-mail ....

Send your order to *Concilium,* **Hymns Ancient and Modern Ltd**
13a Hellesdon Park Road, Norwich NR6 5DR, UK
E-mail: concilium@hymnsam.co.uk
or order online at www.conciliumjournal.co.uk

Customer service information
All orders must be prepaid. Your subscription will begin with the next issue of Concilium. If you have any queries or require Information about other payment methods, please contact our Customer Services department.

www.ingramcontent.com/pod-product-compliance
Ingram Content Group UK Ltd.
Pitfield, Milton Keynes, MK11 3LW, UK
UKHW040237250426
12048UKWH00042B/1559